The Complete Guide to Edible Wild Plants, Mushrooms, Fruits, and Nuts

The Complete Guide to Edible Wild Plants, Mushrooms, Fruits, and Nuts

How to Find, Identify, and Cook Them

Katie Letcher Lyle

THE LYONS PRESS
Guilford, Connecticut
An imprint of The Globe Pequot Press

The Lyons Press is an imprint of The Globe Pequot Press.

Illustrations of pages 31, 55, and 151 from *Wild Food Cookbook* by Frances Hamerstrom are used by permission of the artist, Elva H. Paulson. Illustrations on pages 14, 52, and 132 from *Gather Ye Wild Things* by Susan Tyler Hitchcock are used by permission of the artist, G.E. McIntosh.

The following poems have been reprinted by permission:
"Morels" from *Collected Poems* 1939-1989, published by Charles Scribner's Sons, 1990, copyright © 1990 by William Jay Smith "The Hermit Picks Berries" from *Selected Poems* 1960-1990, by Maxine Kumin, published by W. W. Norton & Co., Inc., copyright © 1972 by Maxine Kumin.

A word of caution:
The Lyons Press, Publishers, recommends that readers consult a variety of field guides to help identify wild plants. As some edible plants have poisonous look-alikes, never eat a plant without positively identifying it as safe. Always taste a small amount of an edible wild plant to determine that you are not allergic to it before committing to a whole plateful. Due to the varied experience and education of the readers, The Lyons Press, Publishers, specifically disclaims any responsibility for injury, sickness, or death from the eating of wild plants and makes no warranties, guarantees, or assurances of any kind.

10 9 8 7 6 5 4 3 2

Printed in the United States of America

ISBN 1-59228-288-1

Library of Congress Cataloging-in-Publication Data is available on file.

For my longtime morelling companion
Burwell Wingfield, and for Janet Lembke,
whose wild crabmeat and wild essays nourish my body
and spirit, and in memory of my friend Marjorie Bendl,
who now forages in greener fields.

CONTENTS

INTRODUCTION

I've been a forager all my life. My earliest foraging memory comes from San Diego, when I was only three.

We had been to the beach, my father and I, and were homeward bound in late afternoon when we crossed Mission Bay at low tide and Daddy spotted lobsters, trapped when the tide went out. All we had to collect them in was my potty, so we waded in and scooped lobsters out of the sandy pools. Three of them, and the pot was bulging. Back at the car, we found it wouldn't start, so we walked to the nearest streetcar line to wait for the next trolley (still in our bathing suits) with the potty containing the indignant lobsters. We rode the crowded trolley home juggling the potty to keep the frantic denizens corralled, to the delight of the other commuters. At home, Mama was outraged that we had made such a scene, had been practically nude in public!

But Daddy winked at me. His face was shining with pleasure, and I savored the delight of being regarded as a maverick. I loved the attention we had attracted; it was most certainly preferable to Mama standing fully dressed, hands on hips, frowning disapprovingly at her two happy, bad kids. To my mother, the worst sin was to make a spectacle of yourself.

So early on, foraging became a source of pleasure; it meant taking a walk out in some gorgeous place; it meant finding some treasure; it meant getting something for nothing. In California, there was always something ripe: We'd stop and gather windfall oranges along the road, olives out of a wild grove, garlic, figs as pink and sweet as candy. Always I felt lucky and happy to be along with Daddy on a treasure hunt.

During World War II, my father went to the Pacific, and my mother, my brother, and I moved back to Virginia and lived with my paternal grandparents, whose lives were very different from the civilized life my mother had in mind for her children. They had a black cook, primitive plumbing, a dog, and lived in a wonderful, dirty old house full of fusty Victorian antiques and pictures of ancestors and saints.

Andaddy, my grandfather, took me in hand, led me down to the creek in the woods down back, and showed me how to catch crawfish and where the watercress grew. On the way home he pointed out an immense pawpaw patch not far from the house, which would have ripe fruits like bananas later on. He handed me sour grass to eat, comparing it to clover so I could always tell the difference, and warned me not to eat buttercups (poisonous, he said). He drove me in his ancient "confounded machine" up in the mountains, where I found wild strawberries and my first case of chiggers. On the way, he told me the world's biggest diamond, over fifty pounds, had been found near here, just over the border in West Virginia, so I should keep an eye out. The people who'd found it had used it as a doorstop for years before they learned it was a diamond, he told me.

In summer, we'd fish for small bass and perch that lived in the Maury River, and I'd get a history lesson about Matthew Fontaine Maury, the Pathfinder of the Seas. Andaddy'd tell me about the big eels that spawned upriver all the way to Lexington until the big dams were built for electricity.

In fall, two days after the first frost, we'd go to shake persimmons out of a tree he knew of, and he taught me how to crack and pick the black walnuts that fell all over the big yard.

I loved it from the first. It was in my blood to forage. Later in my life, I chose my husband for his woodsy ways, and he and I chose our 1867 house at least in part because of the three gigantic hundred-year-old sugar maples in the yard, which we tap early in the spring. In the wet summer of 1969, I taught myself about fungi, and we collected, cataloged, and ate over two hundred different kinds. Our children grew up knowing plants and eating wineberries and puffballs.

Maple syrup, morels, and watercress are all delicacies, and all of them cost dearly when you find them in stores. Yet all are *free* to those who will only go looking for them.

Foraging has got to be good for you; in our world of deadlines and noise and air pollution, the meditative calm of walking in fields or woods is restorative. The gentle exercise is healing. Emerson was right: *Nature is loved by what is best in us.* And the trophy of a basket of mushrooms, a bunch of pungent mint, or a bag of fragrant fresh-ground cornmeal makes you want to crow with pride. In addition, foraging is a pastime that anyone can take up at any age, and one that can last a lifetime. It's a hobby that costs nothing.

One of our children was born with cerebral palsy and mental retardation, yet Jennie has always been able to enjoy our expeditions to the woods, our long walks in search of good things to eat, our forays to a creek after watercress. I am sure she can walk better than she might have without a family committed to being often outdoors, and she takes great pride in knowing her birds, and being able to identify many plants.

In all, foraging is a healthy pursuit, a safe and profitable hobby, a pleasure that the entire family, any family, can enjoy, a treat for visitors, an adventure for any season.

Although foraging may be more easily within the reach of a small-town or rural population than it is for city folk, most cities contain parks and vacant lots. Even if we don't own wild land, we still have access to woods in the form of national forests and national parks. I've personally seen unpicked ripe blackberries in New York City's Central Park, lambs'-quarters growing profusely in a vacant lot in Queens, and mulberries staining the sidewalks of a downtown Baltimore neighborhood where I lived.

Euell Gibbons, the acknowledged American authority on wild foods, has proved beyond a doubt that many wild plants are indeed edible, and even salubrious. However, Gibbons's criterion was edibility; mine is really fine taste. The average, but resourceful, enthusiast can enjoy the fruits of foraging most of the year—all of the year if he or she owns a freezer.

Wild food, of course, grows without insecticides, without human manipulation. Plants at the highway's edge receive the residue from automobile exhaust, so pick a few feet away from roads. Always wash wild food with as much care as you would foods from the supermarket.

Gathering wild food, getting something wonderful for nothing, is one of life's greatest pleasures, and may, if we listen respectfully to the voice of "the folk," enhance health and cure illness. In this book I have given some attention to the folklore of the plants, including medicinal uses, as well as recipes for your delectation. Certainly the early settlers used plants thoughtfully, believing in specific efficacies through observation and contact with aboriginal Americans, as well as relying on the knowledge and plants they brought from Europe. Folk medicine is not to be taken lightly. For instance, it was recorded often that Indians cured cancer by ingesting mayapple; they knew when and how to employ that poisonous plant. By taking folk claims seriously, and testing the mayapple, modern medicine has isolated a cure for testicular cancer from mayapple resin, thus saving thousands of men's lives. When remedies using wild plants are tested by sophisticated pharmaceutical companies, the results are often impressive.

Midwives in the distant past doctored other women and children, and their own menfolk. But beginning in the late medieval period, male physicians trained at European universities refused to use any methods they had not been taught there, and midwifery became second-class medicine. Appalachian midwives have traditionally (but very quietly) prescribed one teaspoon of the dried seeds of Queen Anne's lace in one glass of water, drunk the morning after intercourse, as an effective postcoital method of birth control. Only recently and by accident an archaeologist "rediscovered" this method in an ancient Latin inscription. The two branches of medicine, folk and academic, have only recently begun to share information, and it is exciting to see folk remedies and procedures exonerated.

◼ ABOUT PLANT NAMES

Plants are officially known by their genus and species names, and it's not only a good mental exercise to learn the proper botanical names of the plants you gather and eat, but it will also help prevent confusion. Folk names change from one part of the country to another. Though the tendency in botanical nomenclature is toward uniformity, plant designations change all the time. Thus, species of plants are not entirely fixed either. Separating species and varieties is still an imperfect science.

The problem is not naming, but identifying. Plant identification is about three centuries old; formalized spelling is not that old. Occasionally, different spellings are both correct: *Virginiana and virginica* are both acceptable, and *chinensis* and *sinensis* may both be applied to a plant that was first discovered in China. Standardization is slow, especially as serious botanists still disagree about how to categorize plants, arguing over minute characteristics. In nature, there is simply no finality, especially in a world where botanists believe that we have discovered and classified only about half of the plants that exist. However, when learning about plants, do learn the proper nomenclature. If you tell the emergency room staff you've eaten little red berries and gotten a stomachache, they may not know how to treat you. If you tell them you accidentally ate *Solanum dulcamara,* they will know just what to do for you.

▣ A WORD ABOUT COOKING METHODS

I've found "cooking by process" works best for me. This means learning a basic process, such as preparing soufflés or pizza, and then varying that process according to your own taste, available ingredients, whether you're cutting down on fat, and so on. A simple example of process cooking is rice. The process of cooking rice does not vary often. Measure your rice, then measure twice as much water. Bring that water to a boil, add the rice slowly, bring it to a boil again, reduce the heat to low, cover the pan, and cook it without stirring until the rice has absorbed the water. Easy to do, easy to remember. But you can salt it or not, add a pat of butter or a little oil, some dried herbs or some chopped vegetables, or nothing.

The beauty of this process approach to cooking is that learning ten or twenty basic processes frees you to become a creative cook and to make an endless number of dishes. Once you've learned a process, many variations are possible. I often will give you imprecise amounts of ingredients, because with wild food, you can't always count on having exactly two cups. But also, in most cases, exact amounts make no difference at all in the final product.

In addition, basic recipes, like the one for Mayonnaise, will appear from time to time within these chapters.

So come on! I invite you to the hunt, the gathering, the folklore, the pictures, and the feast.

My warmest thanks to all the friends who made this project such fun: the librarians and friends I asked questions of, those who tried out the recipes, intrepid foragers who went with me, tolerant cronies who put up with my obsessions and cheered me on. They are: Karen Bailey, LuAnn Balfry, Georgianna Brush, Carolyn Cox, Cynthia LaRue, Andy Johnson, Wendy Knick, John Letcher, Peter Letcher, Lisa Mc-Cown and C. Vaughan Stanley of the Washington and Lee University Rare Books Collection, Grace McCrowell, Sally Hill McMillan, Hope Mihalap, General "Jimmy" Morgan, Mario Pellicciaro, Sarah Rorrer,

Edgar Shew, Tommy Spencer, Suzie Thompson, Frances Tolley, Martha Boyden Williams, Chris Wise, Maureen Worth, Rebecca Worth—and as always, my fan club, to whom I'm most grateful—my wonderful children, Cochran and Jennie, and my dear long-suffering husband, Royster.

GEARING UP

You will find foraging an affordable hobby. One needs very little to gather wild food. Jeans or khakis, a long-sleeved shirt, hiking boots or supportive walking shoes (high-top is better than low-top for ankle support and peace of mind near snakes) with good socks, and bug repellent are the only *real* essentials. All your clothes should be washable. (If your jacket brushes against poison ivy, the urushiol will stay on the jacket until it's washed, creating a hazard for anyone who picks it up, handles it, or wears it.) You need to protect your skin not only from insects of all kinds but also from injury that can result from scraping against something thorny, so tuck the jeans into your socks and make sure your neckline is high. Wear your hair up and covered with a cap or hat, and see that your shirtsleeves protect your arms all the way down to your hands. In buggy weather, spray or slather repellent generously on all parts of your body that are still exposed.

I carry year-round in my car trunk several field guides to identify wild greens, wildflowers, fruits, ferns, and fungi. I also keep a supply of paper and plastic bags there, scissors, a sharp knife, a trowel, and heavy garden gloves (the last to gather stinging nettles, which are delicious and chock-full of vitamins), so that at any moment I am ready to pull over and gather anything good I spy by the roadside. If I walk through fields or woods, I carry necessities in a cheap, light nylon backpack to leave my hands free. And I wear a watch because time is fluid, and when I'm gathering morels or blackberries, ginseng or chanterelles, I may go on far beyond time to go home.

A white or very light hat is good to wear because gnats go for the lightest, highest thing around, which is why they like your face instead of, say, your kneecaps. Spraying the hat with insect repellent will help keep them away from your eyes. One of those Thinsulate space-age jackets sold by sporting equipment companies is good to own; it adds almost no weight to your supplies, but in the event of a sudden weather change you'll be grateful to have it. Should you feel uncomfortably hot in all this gear, remember this: If you ever step into ground hornets, as I did once, you'll be glad you're all covered up.

In summer, it's good to shake flowers of sulfur (powdered sulfur, available at any pharmacy) down inside your socks, and to wear long-sleeved garments tight at the neck and wrists to repel chiggers and all ticks. You can also dot yourself with oil of citronella, which smells marvelous and is safe. Bugs apparently don't like sulfur and citrusy things. Some people swear by Avon's Skin-So-Soft bath oil. Avon now puts out in addition a product called Skin-So-Soft Moisturizing Suncare Plus, which contains the bath oil, an SPF of 15, and oil of citronella. I've found another product called T.O.P., "total outdoor protection," that includes citronella and SPF 15 by Biopharm of Bellport, New York. I could write a discourse on all the insect repellents I've tried, including the crushed leaves of a citrus geranium known as mosquito plant (never mind; it doesn't work) and a battery-operated mosquito repellent that whined until I thought I'd go mad—though the mosquitoes seemed unfazed by it—and crushed mint and pennyroyal leaves, boiled orange or lemon rinds, kerosene (my grandfather's favorite), and so on. My dear husband loves to spend the night in the woods in a sleeping bag, and he never gets a bite of any sort. But being a fair and tender lady, I go for Cutters', 6–12, Deep Woods *Off!*, or some other heavy-duty brand of commercial repellent. Whatever you do, you don't want to spend your time in the woods miserably batting at gnats, or come home covered with mosquito or spider bites (and any walk in the woods is sooner or later going to take you through a spiderweb). I once got a spider bite that took a year to heal. Now I'm more careful. And these days, a tick bite can be life threatening. So don't take chances.

I had it years ago on the somewhat questionable authority of my grandfather that snakes detest whistling because it hurts their ears (I *know* they don't have ears, but they *do* have earlike organs that are very sensitive). My fellow mushroom hunter, biologist Dr. Burwell Wingfield of the Virginia Military Institute, confirms that snakes "hear" vibrations, whether they be musical or "felt" through the ground. So just to be on the safe side, I whistle and stomp my way through the woods in summer—and hardly ever encounter a snake. If you give them half a chance, they will try to get out of your way.

Rabid animals are a possible threat, but an unlikely one: Most people would never get bitten if they would only remember to *stay far away from any wild animal that doesn't act wild*. Bands of frothing squirrels attacking and killing unwary humans is a good scenario for a horror film, but it hasn't happened yet that I know of.

There are a few rules that foragers need to bear in mind:

- *If the land you're hunting on isn't yours, first ask permission.* If a stranger came into your yard and began picking your flowers, you'd be incensed.

- *Carefully identify the things you plan to eat.* Learning to identify the wild things that grow in your area is a great pleasure, and not difficult. Peruse your local bookstore or library for field guides to wild plants and mushrooms. In the case of plants, compare not only field characteristics but also the season of growth and the locale. Learn what poisonous plants in your region look like in all seasons. A salad of poison ivy would not set well. Plant, mammal, insect, and bird identification increases the pleasure of walking, even if you never forage. Walking increases your joy in life. The dramatic reduction in walking since the advent of automobiles probably has as much to do with contemporary health problems as air pollution and high-fat diets. Forming a habit of walking every day may be the best possible assurance of a long and healthy life—and a long life doesn't seem desirable to me unless it is healthy.

- *Then you get to gather.* Take what you need, recalling that a lot of wild products freeze well. Treat your produce with care; a flat gathering basket keeps delicate berries, greens, and fungi from crushing those on the bottom, even if it's not as convenient to carry as plastic bags are.

- *Clean wild food well.* Nothing ruins the appetite so much as biting down on grit, or finding a stinkbug crawling around in your salad. Worse than that would be getting liver flukes from polluted water. The method for cleaning watercress (see page 40) is necessary because the plants grow in running water, and any running water these days might be polluted. For all other greens, multiple rinses in fresh, clean tap water are sufficient. Mushrooms need to be scrupulously cleaned, as they all grow up *through* soil (and often manure) and may thus retain some clinging bits. Berries need gentle washing to float out any critters, which seem to enjoy them as much as we do. Other fruits just need rinsing off.

- *When you get home, clean yourself well also.* Search diligently for ticks, both the big ones and those the size of poppy seeds. *Both* now can carry, in addition to Rocky Mountain spotted fever, Lyme disease and a new bacterial disease, HGE (human granulocytic ehrlichiosis), which is even more deadly. Inspect your entire body, shower well, soaping thoroughly in case you've brushed against poison oak or ivy, and inspect your body again after bathing. Wash your clothes before wearing them again as a final precaution against poison oak or ivy.

• After you've *gained permission and identified, gathered, and cleaned wild food,* use it just like tame food.

• You might want to *keep records* of where and when you found that asparagus or the black chanterelles, so you can return next week or next year.

• Finally, *be a good neighbor.* Whenever possible, take along a trash bag and help the environment out where you see the need.

If worse comes to worst, and you find nothing on your walk, you can always stop by the store on the way home and substitute something from the produce department. Beet tops, radish tops, and turnip tops, usually discarded, are great for salads, so if you use them, you're doing a sort of foraging.

Just a word about cooking utensils: I will assume that everyone owns a blender, a big colander, a salad spinner, kitchen scissors, a potato masher or a ricer (a heavy-duty strainer for mashing potatoes, apples, berries, etc., and separating the cooked flesh from skin, seeds, and cores), a food processor, and a big enamel or stainless steel kettle with a tight-fitting lid. (I avoid aluminum cookware, as the jury is still not in on the dangers of aluminum absorption leading to Alzheimer's disease.) All these items are helpful and in some cases necessary for cooking wild foods, not to mention everything else.

GREEN THINGS

*Most of us are still related to our native fields as the naviga-
tor to undiscovered islands in the sea. We can any afternoon
discover a new fruit there, which will surprise us by the beauty
of its sweetness.*

—Henry David Thoreau

There's an exciting and overlooked category of leafy things not as widely used as Boston lettuce, romaine, and iceberg. They are wild, and they include a great many greens both better tasting and more nutritious than store-bought lettuce. In addition, there are asparagus, fiddleheads, and milkweed, as useful and delicious as green beans and broccoli.

Spring is the best time for hunting wild greens, though several are also edible later in the summer, or even year-round. Any access to a field or pasture, or even the edge of a country road, will surely yield several delicious and healthful varieties of greens in all but the snowiest months. The ones I include here are by no means the only edible wild greens, but I believe these are the tastiest.

▣ ASPARAGUS

Asparagus *(Asparagus officinalis)* may derive from the word *asper,* meaning "rough," or *aspergere,* meaning "to scatter." It has been long known throughout Appalachia as sparrowgrass, or sparrergrass, obviously through some misapprehension that made sense to the hearer: Sparrows (which name may be applied to any nondescript little birds) love the bright red seeds that ripen in mid- to late summer.

DESCRIPTION, HABITAT, AND SEASON

Asparagus is a light, bluish green plant with fernlike, feathery fronds; it stands three to four feet tall, and this year's shoots grow out of and around last year's skeletal stalks. Asparagus, with its perennial roots and its annual stalks, grows wild along country roads, in old fields where fences used to run, and along present fencerows. This is because birds eat the berries, then sit resting on fences, where they excrete the undigested parts, including the seeds, which take root and grow. Asparagus also grows randomly in meadows and weedy areas. It is a plant of Temperate Zones. Wild asparagus is exactly the same as commercially available asparagus; sometimes the stalks may have a purplish tint and sometimes they are pure green. (The French sometimes blanch, or fade, asparagus to whiten it. This kind of blanching covers the stalks for several days prior to cutting to prevent light from hitting the plant and causing photosynthesis, which turns plants green.) Its growing season is late spring, when the stalks appear. If the stalks are not picked, they go to seed and put out feathery fronds—but the plant shows more obviously later, in the fall, when the slender shoots have become lacy fronds and produce the red berries containing the seeds. Therefore, it's useful to identify asparagus plants in the autumn, take note of where they are, and then in the spring go looking for the tender young shoots among last year's dead stalks. Asparagus is hardy, and continues to put up shoots from its deep roots year after year, even if discouraged by the democratic slaughter of the highway mowers. The plant tends to grow among other long grasses in roadside ditches, making it hard to see when it's at the edible stage. When you find the stalks, snap them off a foot or so from the top. If they are less than seven or eight inches high, snap them off at the ground. Occasionally, if the summer is long, you can find a second growth of shoots late in that season, but it never produces as many as you find in spring.

HISTORY AND LORE

Although asparagus is ubiquitous in moderate climates, it is like the legendary selkie; it was once a sea plant, growing near the ocean in sandy soil, and now lives among land plants. It is a plant included in that honorable, much sought, but mysterious group known as aphrodisiacs.

R E C I P E S

In April to June, when asparagus is plentiful, save some for future use by another process called blanching. This time the word means submerging something, usually vegetables, for 1 minute in boiling water, then into ice water for 1 minute, and freezing it for future use. This blanching stops the enzyme action by which any plant continues its steady process of maturation and, finally, decline. Freezing alone is not sufficient to retard decomposition.

When you want to cook the frozen asparagus (or any frozen vegetable), do not thaw it first. Plunge it into 1 inch of boiling water, and cook only until it is thawed.

To cook fresh asparagus, cut spears about 8 inches from the top, and steam them in $\frac{1}{2}$ cup water for 1 to 2 minutes only, so they stay crisp. Eat them plain, or dribbled with melted butter, olive oil, or lemon juice, or a combination of all three. Asparagus is also fine to nibble raw, or chop raw into salads.

Asparagus Pizza
(A good way to use a few asparagus stalks.
Yields 1 pizza, about 14" across.)

Prepare pizza dough according to the directions on pages 178–180. Bake it for 3 minutes in an oven preheated to 450°F. Remove, and lightly brush the top with olive oil. Put a very light layer of tomato sauce on first, then scatter 1" slices of fresh raw asparagus over the top. Scatter with 1 or 2 cloves finely minced garlic, salt and pepper, oregano, end with a light smattering of mozzarella or provolone cheese, and bake until its color pleases you.

Asparagus and Pasta
(Serves four to six.)

Cook 1 lb. of ziti or mostaccioli pasta (or any other pasta) until al dente ("to the tooth," or still a bit resistant). While the pasta is boiling, heat ¼ cup olive oil in a skillet, add 8 chopped garlic cloves and ¼ tsp., more or less, red pepper flakes. Sauté 2 minutes, stirring occasionally. Add what asparagus you have, up to 1 lb., the spears cut about the same length as the pasta, and stir-fry for 2 minutes. (This differs from sautéing in that you stir continously.) Salt and pepper the asparagus, and toss with drained pasta. Grate 1 cup or so of Parmesan cheese over the top, and serve immediately.

▣ CHICORY

Chicory *(Cichorium intybus)* is a familiar sight along country roads, and a plant generally neglected these days. "Chicory" is an anglicization of the Arabic, *chicouryeh.* The Romans knew the plant as *cichorium,* which in turn was taken from the Greek.

DESCRIPTION, HABITAT, AND SEASON

Although this deep-rooted perennial is most easily identifiable by its profuse summer daisylike blue flowers, chicory is best used as food for its leaves in the spring, before it flowers, or for its root in the fall. When chicory first comes out in the spring it has oblong basal foliage that forms, at ground level, a loose head of dark green leaves that have a slightly bitter but pleasant taste, and are excellent salad greens. Europeans cherish this green, and cultivate it, but in this country we must gather it wild. Chicory is a close kin to dandelion, as is evidenced by the upper, deeply lobed leaves. The spring leaves of the two plants can be used interchangeably, adding a slightly bitter piquancy to salads.

After flowering, in the autumn, is when to dig chicory root, which makes a very good beverage on its own, or can be added to ground coffee. But you must locate the plant by its blue summer-morning flowers, then return to dig the root after the flowers are gone.

HISTORY AND LORE

Chicory was originally native to Arabic countries, from which it was introduced to Europe. Like many of our wild plants, it was first brought to North America from Europe by early colonists, then escaped to dot our fields, empty city lots, and roadsides with its cheery blue flowers.

Among the ancient Romans, chicory enjoyed a reputation as a cure not only for jaundice but also for anemia, infertility, and liver ailments. It is still said to be tonic and restorative.

Linnaeus once planted a flower bed in his native Uppsala, Sweden, to act as a reliable clock, as he had determined that different flowers blossomed at different times. In midsummer at that northern latitude, Linnaeus's chicory blooms opened at 5 A.M. and closed at 10 P.M. on sunny days. In Virginia at midsummer, it's closer to 7 A.M. and 7 P.M.

RECIPES

Roast Chicory Root

Chicory roots, scrubbed clean, can be boiled and eaten, and are a popular vegetable in Lebanon and other countries of Eurasia. In America, chicory roots were substituted during the Civil War for coffee. To use them this way, dig the roots out in early fall. To get the whole root out, you may have to dig as deep as 2 feet. Wash and clean each root well, and cut it with a machete or very sharp knife into chunks or thick slices. Roast the root in a medium-low oven (about 280°F) until the pieces turn from white to brown, about 1 hour.

When they are cool, grind them up to the consistency of coffee grounds. Add 1 tsp. ground root to each Tbsp. of coffee grounds, filtering, dripping, or perking the roots along with the coffee. Or prepare the root alone, without coffee, (using 1 Tbsp. for each cup) for a healthy caffeine-free hot drink. So popular was the taste that dark-roast coffee with chicory to this day remains the standard New Orleans brew.

> Dandelion and chicory leaves can be blanched if you prefer. To blanch (whiten) a plant, you must either cover the plants with bushel baskets or plugged flowerpots and leave them to grow in the dark for several days, or dig up the roots and replant them in a dark cellar. The folklore is that blanching renders any plant less bitter, but if it does, it is only by a matter of a degree. And it's a lot of trouble.

▨ DANDELIONS

Dandelions *(Taraxacum officinale)* are well known to adorn grassy areas and fields everywhere, and are a bane to millions of shortsighted folks who insist on perfectly green lawns instead of lawns dotted with yellow. The Latin name translates as "the official medical dandelion." A plant that has the word *officinale* in its name was once used officially for medicine. The English name is simply a version of the French *dent de leon,* or "tooth of the lion," from the deeply indented leaf shape, not the sunny flower.

Description, Habitat, and Season

As an edible plant, the dandelion is good only in early spring before the cheerful, bright yellow flowers bloom. The leaves, deeply lobed and bright green, are a forager's delight, and have a pleasant, slightly bitter taste. (After the plant has flowered, the leaves become tough and unpleasantly bitter.) In Europe dandelion leaves are popular in spring salads. Dandelion leaves may also be used as a potherb (that is, cooked).

History and Lore

Apothecaries of the sixteenth century called dandelions *Herba urinaria*. Even today the plant is prized as a diuretic.

Dandelion leaf tea was drunk by American Indians as a spring tonic, and it does have large amounts of iron and vitamins C and A, which the human body needs after months of diminished sunlight. The hollow stems exude a bitter white latex that is said to soothe bee stings, dissolve warts, and heal sores. Eating the leaves is even supposed to help ease rheumatism.

R E C I P E S

Although dandelion wines still enjoy some popularity, dandelion is best employed as a salad green. Like chicory root, which it is closely related to, dandelion root gathered in autumn may be cleaned, slow-roasted, and ground for a safe, caffeine-free hot beverage, or mixed with coffee.

Traditional Dandelion Salad
(Serves four.)

Fry a few strips of bacon until crisp, then crumble and set aside. Drain off some of the bacon grease, leaving about 2 Tbsp. In the hot skillet, lay a great mound of fresh, washed, wet young dandelion leaves (they will spatter), and stir over the heat until the leaves are coated with the fat, just 1 minute or so. Sprinkle with salt, pepper, and vinegar, add the bacon and 1 or 2 chopped hard-boiled eggs, and serve at once. The salad should be barely wilted. (Draining off the bacon drippings, or most of them, would modernize this old recipe.)

Italian-Style
Nouvelle Dandelion Salad
(Serves four.)

Heat a few Tbsp. of olive oil with a few cloves of garlic crushed or minced, a couple of inches of anchovy paste, 1 Tbsp. or so of capers, and a handful of pine nuts. Mix the ingredients well, and heat and stir them together just for 1 or 2 minutes, until the pine nuts begin to brown. Then add the washed greens to the hot skillet and stir and toss for 1 minute or so, until the leaves are coated. Wilt, but don't cook, the leaves.

▣ FIDDLEHEADS

Fiddleheads are the coiled tender tips or sprouts of several different kinds of ferns. The ones most commonly eaten in America are cinnamon fern (*Osmunda cinnamomea*), bracken (*Pteridium aquilinum* or "eagle feather"), and ostrich fern (*Pteretis struthiopteris* or "Knotty Feathered"). The second and third derive from the Greek *pteron*, "feather" or "wing," and describe the feathery stalks of ferns. The cinnamon fern is named for Osmunder, the Saxon war god. Ferns are among the oldest plants on earth. The common name fiddleheads comes from their resemblance to, well, the heads of fiddles, the tops of the violins that are carved to appear coiled.

DESCRIPTION, HABITAT, AND SEASON

In order to enjoy these vegetables, which are commercially canned by several food processing companies, you should identify the fern beds the year before, so that you can return in early spring and watch for the emergence of the tender young fiddleheads. This is not hard: Though ferns all look alike to the casual observer, they are not at all the same up close. So buy a good fern guide, and take a trek in the woods when the leaves are out, and soon you will be an expert at spotting ferns and even identifying some of them. Then all you need do is remember where your ferns grow, and return in early spring before they uncurl their little heads and their feathery displays emerge.

Cinnamon fern is a large (around three feet high), common, coarse fern distinguished from other ferns by the late spring gold-green leaves that turn the color of cinnamon. Cinnamon fern likes damp places, and puts out fiddleheads that are large, with silvery white, fine hairs.

Bracken fern is also a very common, strong, coarse fern that grows in colonies to about three feet tall in fields, burned areas, sandy areas, and generally on high ground. The leaves are wavy, dark green, and flatten out horizontally at the top; each stem produces three equal leaves of subleaflets. Its fiddleheads thus grow in three parts, curled tight, covered with silvery hair.

Ostrich fern is large, about five feet tall, and arches gracefully like ostrich feathers. Ostrich fern spreads easily, and appears in dense colonies in wet habitats, by creeks and in marshy land. Ostrich fern is common in the East, less common in other parts of the country. It is a dark blackish green, turning dark brown in winter, often matting stretches of stream banks.

HISTORY AND LORE

Ferns are among our most ancient plants. Often fern fossils are discovered buried deep in rock layers. Brontosaurs and other vegetable-eating dinosaurs nibbled fiddleheads. Ferns have been employed medically for endless ailments as far ranging as tapeworms, baldness, coughs, and dysentery.

RECIPES

Fiddleheads require careful cleaning of the scales or hairs, and cooking. Once cleaned and steamed to tenderness, they are delicious hot or cold. Ostrich fern and cinnamon fern fiddleheads should be steamed only as long as it takes to tenderize them. Bracken fiddleheads require longer cooking, and some sources suggest changing the water 3 times during boiling, but I never do this. I like their distinctive flavor.

French Fiddleheads

Wash fiddleheads (about ½ cup for each diner). They need to be blanched quickly (dunked in boiling water for 1 minute) then rinsed in cold water. Then gently boil them in fresh water until just tender, about as long as you'd cook string beans. Serve them with lemon butter when they are cooked but still crisp.

Chilled Fiddleheads

Wash fiddleheads. (Allow ½ cup for each person.) Blanch them as above, boil them as above, then place them briefly in cold water to keep them from getting soggy. Drain, and marinate them in Salad Dressing (see pages 176–77) overnight in the refrigerator for a wonderful addition to a salad, or a green worthy of center stage on any table. They also are great chilled with homemade Mayonnaise (see page 176).

Fiddlehead Soup
(Serves four.)

Wash and clean 1 or 2 cups fiddleheads. Beat 2 eggs with about ⅓ cup fresh lemon juice. Heat 1 quart or so seasoned stock to just boiling. You can use consommé, beef broth, chicken broth, veal broth, or vegetable broth. (See pages 175–76 for basic broth process.) First add fiddleheads to broth and simmer 5 minutes. Remove about 1 cup simmering broth and stir into egg-lemon mix. Then turn the whole mix into the pot, stir well, and remove at once from the heat. Stir again, and serve at once, distributing the fiddleheads among the servings more or less evenly.

▣ LAMBS'-QUARTERS

Lambs'-quarters (sometimes spelled lamb-squarters) *(Chenopodium album)* may be the greatest treasure you'll ever find. Its name in Latin means "goose-footed plant" (hence another nickname, goosefoot). *Album* refers to the white "bloom" or dust that looks like talcum powder on the leaf surfaces close to the stem. Pigweed, as it is dismissively called in Appalachia for the animal's preference for it, is a veritable treasure. In some places it's known as wild spinach. Its folk name lambs'-quarters probably comes from its affinity for pastures, or lambs' quarters.

DESCRIPTION, HABITAT, AND SEASON

Chenopodium is one foot to three feet tall, has roughly diamond-shaped or triangular leaves, and is powdered with coarse, grainy particles of white, so that it looks dusty. Sometimes the stalks are streaked with red. *Chenopodium* grows everywhere vegetables will grow, plus lots of other places. It's a grayish spire-shaped weed that likes the edges of gardens, barnyards, and unguarded parts of your backyard, as well as fields and pathways, and . . . well, once you've identified it, you'll see how ubiquitous it is. From early spring all the way to first frost, you can gather and use young leaves from plants that are between six and sixteen inches tall. (Any taller, and the leaves may be tough. In taller plants, strip the leaves off the stalk.) In an irony of nature, lambs'-quarters loves to move into spinach patches as well as other parts of gardens. Gardeners I know spend a lot of time trying to rid their spinach (and other) patches of it, even though it's every bit as delicious as the vegetables intentionally being grown. Euell Gibbons reports that in Hawaii and California, its cheerful willingness to take root and grow has caused farmers distress.

HISTORY AND LORE

Pigweed is undaunted by the unkind treatment it receives. It's willing to grow anywhere, it's full of nutrients, and hardly anyone you ask these days has ever even heard that it's edible, much less delicious. It has exceptional amounts of vitamins A and C, only a half cup or so providing the daily needed amount of both, as well as fiber, of course, and also calcium. My vegetable-growing neighbor brings it to me with amusement, while worrying about his spinach. One time I made spinach soup and lambs'-quarters soup with the same ingredients, only changing the greens. My neighbor agreed with me that the lambs'-quarters soup was better, but habit is so strong that he still sows, tends, and weeds his spinach carefully each year while the lambs'-quarters, without his interference, thrives exuberantly at the edge of his garden, and year after year only I eat it.

RECIPES

Use lambs'-quarters any way that you would spinach, but strip the leaves off the stalks. Clean the leaves well in 2 or 3 rinsings of water, to rinse off the bloom on the leaves.

Lambs'-Quarters Bisque or Soup
(Serves four.)

This is just about the best you will ever taste. Wash and rewash a big bunch of leaves stripped from their stalks. The leaves will collapse as soon as heat reaches them. To make 1 quart or so of wonderful soup, sauté or steam a bunch of the wet washed leaves the size of a basketball in 2 or 3 Tbsp. butter for 1 minute or so. You can add some chopped onion, too. Stir in 2 to 3 Tbsp. flour to make a roux. Slowly add about 3 cups chicken or beef broth, canned or homemade (see method on page 175), stir while you bring it to a boil, and add one of the following: 1 block cream cheese (you can use either a 3-oz. or an 8-oz. block, depending on how creamy you want your bisque to be), 1 cup sour cream, 8 oz. heavy whipping cream. You can turn the bisque into plain old soup by adding milk instead, which will save calories, too. Blend the mixture briefly in a blender, taste and correct seasoning, then keep hot until you are ready to serve, but do not boil again. Naturally you could make this soup with other greens, too, including fiddleheads.

Lambs'-Quarters with Potatoes
(Serves four.)

Gather an armful of lambs'-quarters and wash well. Place in a large pot, sprinkle with salt, and steam until wilted. In a second pot, place some cubed potatoes, salt, pepper, and a spoonful of bacon drippings, oil, or a little butter. Add 1 cup water and bring to the boiling point. Pour wilted greens on top of potatoes, cover, and cook until potatoes are done. Traditionally, this is served in Missouri with pork sausage.

▧ LAND CRESS

Land cress (*Barbarea vulgaris* or *B. verna*), a member of the mustard family, has a doubly insulting Latin name: It is "barbarous" and "vulgar," and its alternate species name implies a "spring barbarian." Some sources say it is named for St. Barbara, whose annual day is in mid-December. It grows all year if the ground is not frozen and is wet enough. This plant is known by a bewildering variety of folk names, so be

sure to learn the Latin name to avoid confusion. It is also called rocket, arugula, upland cress, winter cress, creesy greens, creesies, Croesus greens (because it's worth more than gold to your body, maybe?), and (erroneously) wild mustard. (*Eruca vesicaria,* the commercial arugula, has deeply lobed leaves and a zippy flavor similar to both land cress and mustard.)

DESCRIPTION, HABITAT, AND SEASON

Land cress grows in full sun out from its center like a rocket, hence one of its folk names. Its shape is the best way to identify this plant. The roundish, smooth, deeply lobed, dark green, glossy leaves grow outward while staying near the ground.

It can be found from earliest spring through the summer and on into fall. Even in winter, a warm wet spell sometimes brings it out. Found everywhere in the Temperate Zone, the perennial habitats of land cress include city lots as well as country pastures, along mountain creeks, and in parks, in wet rich, sandy, or waste soil. In early summer it has small yellow cruciform flowers. Once past spring, land cress gets a bit tough, but only requires a few more minutes' cooking time. The plant can be eaten until the blooms form; after that it tastes bitter.

R E C I P E S

Barbarea is related to broccoli, and when it buds in early summer, the buds can be steamed quickly and eaten just like broccoli. It's a green that needs cooking, in my estimation, though many folks eat it raw in salads.

Greens and Pot Likker
(Serves four to six.)

Fall greens are darker, tougher, and stronger-flavored than spring greens, for the most part, and respond well to the taming effects of heat. For a wonderful feast, gather about a gallon of fall greens like land cress, wild mustard, or a combination of greens. Cut or tear them into pieces if they are big. Remove any tough stems. In a big pan bring 1 quart water to a boil. Add 1 tsp. or more salt. You can also cook the greens with a small amount of smoked meat for seasoning (ham skin, a ham hock, 1 or 2 slices of bacon, or a small piece of smoked ham). If you use meat, boil it alone for 15 to 30 minutes, covered. Add clean greens to the pot, and boil covered until tender, about 20 more minutes. The tougher the greens, the longer they will take to cook. Taste them sooner rather than later: Don't overcook them. Drain. Discard the smoked meat, but save the liquid! Serve the greens alone or with sliced hard-boiled eggs and a sprinkling of malt vinegar. For a different taste, toss them with a little butter and lemon juice. The liquid, known in Appalachia as pot likker for its sublime taste, holds any vitamins that the cooking has leached out of the greens. It is served in teacups, and drunk like tea.

Traditionally, greens, pot likker, and corn bread made up the entire meal for country folks. Today it's still eaten as a hearty and satisfying supper. The corn bread was (though not in our house) dipped into the pot likker, or even crumbled into it. My mother, a Philadelphian, felt it generous to even allow us to *eat* corn bread and greens; dunking was way beyond her limit. (See Country Corn bread, page 144.)

▨ MILKWEED

Milkweed *(Asclepias syriaca)* is a delicious early-summer vegetable, and vastly overlooked in the civilized world. Its Latin name is the same as the Latin god of medicine, *Asclepias*, and *syriaca* may suggest its origin was Syria. It's sometimes called butterfly weed, or butterfly milkweed, and I've heard folks call it pleurisy root. Its folk name comes from the milky, sticky sap that the stem yields when cut or picked.

DESCRIPTION, HABITAT, AND SEASON

Milkweed is likely to inhabit any pastures and fields, waste places, and roadside ditches. It grows in full sun, and is often found in enormous patches. Sometimes whole fields are full of it.

This three-foot North American native plant grows on a hardy stalk. The leaves are dark glossy green, slightly wavy, with a white midvein. They are lance shaped and four to six inches long. Milkweed flowers grow in rounded umbels and are most often whitish purple, with a greenish tinge. You can identify a patch of milkweed when its sweet purple blooms make it stand out, in early summer, and return each year. If you can find them, the youngest shoots in spring grow to six or seven inches high and can be used like asparagus (blanched first for a minute in rapidly boiling water). The buds in late spring are delicious before they open; they look rather like small broccoli heads, and I think they're at least as tasty as broccoli. The buds that blossom in summer are purple and fragrant, attracting butterflies, and they, too, are a fine vegetable.

HISTORY AND LORE

Milkweed traditionally was used to treat infections of the respiratory system both in North America and in Europe. Milkweed seed, when it has burst, is light and fulsome like goose down or cotton, and once was used in Appalachia as a stuffing in vests and coverlets. Milkweed seed was used in World War II as a substitute for real kapok in life jackets before man-made fillers were invented.

R E C I P E S

Although some people eat all parts of the plant, I recommend only the shoots, unopened buds, and blossoms (avoiding the leaves and the pods).

Boiled Milkweed

All three stages need to be washed, then parboiled for 1 minute in 3 different courses of boiling water to wash out the bitter, sticky sap. Then boil shoots, buds, or blossoms 3 or 4 minutes in a fourth pot of boiling water. When done, they can be tossed with a lump of butter and a squeeze of lemon juice, and you have a delicate vegetable that will charm your taste buds.

▨ MUSTARD

Mustard (*Brassica* varieties) is so ubiquitous that some kind is available nearly all year even in supermarkets, and some variety of it, usually several, may be found in grasslands everywhere in this country. *Brassica* is the Latin word for "cabbage," which belongs to the same family. In the South, wild mustard grows everywhere in fields and pastures, and is called simply greens. In other places it is called charlock, from the Old English name of the plant. One variety, *B. juncea*, was brought here by English settlers but is now wild throughout temperate America.

DESCRIPTION, HABITAT, AND SEASON

When it is in bloom, whole fields turn bright yellow with the close-growing, four-petaled flowers. Up close, mustard blossoms look like little gold crosses. Each blossom has six stamens, four long, two short. Although the various dozen or so mustards we have in this country differ somewhat, all mustard leaves are serrated, dark purple-green, deeply lobed, lyre shaped, and often softly prickly along the main leaf vein underneath. The stem is soft and prickly as well. The plant grows as tall as thirty inches. It's a pesty weed most places it grows. There's hardly a playing field, meadow, golf course, riverbank, or roadside without its share of mustard, so it's available to almost anyone. We gather it from spring through late fall.

RECIPES

Mustard's nippy flavor enhances any salad, though it is at its best used as a pot green. It's tender in the spring, bolts early, tough in summer when it's flowering yellow, and somewhat peppery, or biting, in the fall. At our house we eat this country relative of kale, kohlrabi, cabbage, and rape year-round.

Mustard Greens

Past the tender spring growth, use mustard only as a potherb. Wash it well, and cook with only the water that clings to the leaves. Cook it slowly, covered, for 20 minutes, taste it, and cook longer if necessary. Avoid the flowers, for they're bitter. I like to add a bit of "side meat" (unsmoked bacon), or a slice or two of bacon, a hambone, or a ham hock, though it isn't necessary. Mustard is rich in calcium and vitamins A and C. Its seeds, ground to a fine flour and mixed with wine, vinegar, pepper, horseradish, and sometimes even with Jack Daniel's whiskey, are a popular condiment, and are often used whole in pickles. Once cooked, season with a splash of vinegar, a bit of butter, perhaps a sliced hard-boiled egg.

POKE

Pokeweed *(Phytolacca decandra* or *P. americana)* is also known as poke, skoke, garget, and pigeonberry. Its Latin name means "crimson plant with ten stamens." Pokeberries were once the favorite food of the enormous flocks of passenger pigeons that darkened the skies over the eastern states during their seasonal migrations. (The last known member of the species, which was hunted to extinction, died in a Cincinnati zoo in 1939.)

DESCRIPTION, HABITAT, AND SEASON

To best locate poke for spring picking of the tender shoots, look for it in late summer when the plant is brilliantly colored and dramatically visible in the landscape.

Poke is an easily recognizable green that grows profusely in poor land, unimproved depleted soil, recent clearings, and roadsides throughout the eastern United States, from the Tropics northward throughout the Temperate Zone. It grows six feet or higher, with bright green alternate wavy leaves, a red-streaked or scarlet stem, white to pinkish flowers in late spring, and long loose clusters (racemes) of *toxic* shiny, dark purple berries that develop in late summer and stay into the winter. In late summer, the stem gets redder, and often the entire plant turns a wonderful fuchsia or sunset red. It grows also in wastelands in parts of the western United States, and even in Hawaii. Poke is a striking plant in any landscape.

The whole plant is highly toxic, containing a saponin mixture called phytolaccatoxin—except for the young tender shoots and leaves in early spring, which are often eaten as the first spring green in the southern mountains. Locate the plant in the autumn, or you may miss the shoots among the other spring greens. As they mature, the shoots (any more than seven inches tall) develop the substances toxic to man. Many birds and other animals safely eat pokeberries.

HISTORY AND LORE

Poke has been used for ink, as a dye, and in cures for cancer and arthritis by American Indians. An arthritis cure that a ninety-year-old Missouri man told me of in one of my Elderhostel folklore classes included poke. His father, a country physician, became locally famous in Missouri and some neighboring states at the end of the last century for his arthritis potion, whose formula he kept secret. It worked, according to my informant, nearly all of the time, and facilitated some truly miraculous-seeming cures. It contained, as far as he can remember, only whiskey and pokeberries (well known to the doctor to be poisonous), and was deep purple. My friend recalls seeing people walk who before had been unable to, watching his father's patients' limbs and joints straighten out. But he had no idea when the berries were gathered, whether they were crushed or added whole, if whiskey was the only other ingredient, in what proportions the brew was made, how often it was drunk, or how much per dose. Sadly, now he, too, is dead.

R E C I P E S

Poke shoots are cut at ground level when no more than 7 inches high, parboiled, drained, then cooked until tender in a second water. They are tasty and have a fair amount of vitamin C.

Old-Fashioned Appalachian Poke Sallet

Take a mess of poke shoots, wash them, and chop them coarsely. Boil them for 20 minutes. Meanwhile, fry some pork fatback in a skillet and remove it to drain. Keep the fatback hot. Drain the poke, salt it, and fry it for 5 minutes in the leftover grease. Serve the fried poke with the fried pork and some Corn Bread (see page 144). Sprinkle cider vinegar on the greens and drink buttermilk with it if you want the whole experience.

Fried Poke

Flour up the parboiled young *stalks (no higher than 7 inches)* and fry them in a small amount of bacon fat (or some other less sinful fat). They are said by some to taste just like asparagus. Or flour up the par-boiled young *leaves (just the ones on the early stalks)* and fry them; they are reputed to taste like fish. To me, poke tastes only like itself, and is delicious in its own right.

▩ SORREL

Sorrel *(Rumex acetosa)* and wood sorrel *(Oxalis montana)* are two unrelated plants that grow in yards and meadows everywhere, looking like arrows *(Rumex)* and clover or trefoil *(Oxalis)*. *Oxalis* is the Greek word for "wood sorrel," as *rumex* is the Latin name for "sorrel." *Acetosa* derives from the Latin *acetum,* "vinegar." Both plants are tangy to the palate, which gives them both the common nickname of sour grass. Either one adds greatly to the flavor of soups and salads. The word *sorrel* comes from an old French word, *sur,* meaning "sour."

DESCRIPTION, HABITAT, AND SEASON

Both sorrels like poor soil, so they may be found in uncultivated fields, old lawns, the edges of gardens. Both grow in Temperate Zones of the Northern Hemisphere. The *Oxalis* sorrel is the true shamrock, a low plant with three split leaves much like clover. It is native to the British Isles, but like so many of our wild plants, was introduced by the early colonists. The *Rumex* sorrel is a perennial that grows to three feet or more, the arrow-shaped leaves about four inches long. In the summer, this plant flowers toward the top with small, loose reddish-brownish flowers that last until autumn. Once the flowers bloom, the leaves are too tough to eat.

Both sorrels love to nudge your garden flowers out of the way to grow. Sorrels are found wherever and whenever grass grows, or from early spring throughout the summer and into fall, and are impressively rich in vitamin C. They also contain oxalic acid and oxalate salts, which in large quantities can be poisonous. Nonetheless, sorrel has been safely used for at least six centuries as a soup and salad green in reasonably small quantities.

R E C I P E S

Sorrel as a spring salad green should be used in combination with other greens, and probably no more than 25 percent of your salad should be sorrel. We eat it until frost, though the later the season, the tougher and stronger the plant.

Sorrel Soup, 1898
(Serves four.)

This is from page 6 of my grandmother Letcher's handwritten cookbook, which she started as a bride in 1898. You'll need: 2 Tbsp. butter, 1 pint sorrel, 1 quart soup stock, yolks of 2 eggs, salt and pepper to taste. Put the butter in a saucepan, set it on the fire, and as soon as it's melted, put the sorrel in, and stir 1 minute. Then add the stock, salt, and pepper; boil 3 minutes. Beat the yolks lightly, put them into the tureen, pour the boiling soup over gradually, stirring all the while until thoroughly mixed. Serve with croutons.

◼ STINGING NETTLES

Stinging nettles *(Urtica dioica)* are a delicious wild green, an unlikely food in that they certainly *feel* poisonous, with their thousands of tiny hypodermic needles on the leaves and stems that puncture your skin when you brush against them. *Urtica* is the Latin name for the plant, from *uro,* "I burn," and *dioica* is a Greek word meaning "of two houses." Here it means the plant is unisexual, with male and female flowers in separate parts of the inflorescence, or bloom.

DESCRIPTION, HABITAT, AND SEASON

The plants are dull green and square stemmed, with coarse-toothed, bristly, heart-shaped leaves and small clusters of greenish yellow flowers. They stand a foot or two high on straight stalks. You find nettles along roadsides, on waste ground and in pastures, and around old house sites, from Canada to the Virginias, also throughout the Midwest and even in California. They grow in spring, often in huge patches. You'll want to remember or record where they are so you can return next year to the same places. If in doubt, a loving touch will assure you that you have the right plant.

Only the tender tops (stems and leaves) of nettles in the spring are good to eat; just cut the stalks off no farther down than a foot. Later in the year, even though they continue to put out new plants with apparently tender tops, they are full of tiny crystals that make them gritty and unpleasant. Thus only one picking a year, in any one patch, early to late spring, is my rule. Gather them carefully, with heavy gloves and scissors or a sharp knife.

HISTORY AND LORE

The Romans cultivated nettles, as they proved to be one of the most effective plants for alleviating the miseries of rheumatism. In past times, arthritis and rheumatism sufferers underwent applications of stinging nettles for relief. Today that treatment of one pain to mask another (lotions with capsaicin, the hot stuff of peppers, is one) is called counterirritant. In addition, the fresh stinging leaves are said to stanch bleeding quickly.

A folk adage has it that nettles brewed into tea will "melt fat" from corpulent people. It's worth a try, and even if you don't get thin, you might derive other general health benefits from "taking" nettles.

R E C I P E S

Not only are nettles delicious, they are also extremely high in vitamins A and C. Cooking them quickly converts the formic acid into a digestible protein. Wash them with rubber gloves on, by dousing them up and down in a sinkful of water.

Steamed Nettles

Gather and wash a large bunch of nettles—they cook down—then place them directly into a pot with ¼ cup steaming water in the bottom. Nettles only need about 15 minutes of steaming in a covered kettle, and like magic, the sting has vanished, and they are ready to eat. The greens are delicious with a bit of melted butter and a burst of lemon juice. Drink the pot liquor (the water left when they are done) for its wonderful taste and for the benefit from the minerals that have leached into it. It's better for you than a vitamin pill.

Creamed Nettles

I once ran heedless into a large patch of nettles in pursuit of a neighbor's child's ball. I was barefoot and stuck in the middle of the patch before I became aware of them. I had to turn around and retreat the same way I'd come, adding insult to injury. Their formic acid sting (the same thing that ants sting with) was painful for several hours, finally cooling down to a severe itch, then going away. Though painful, they are not dangerous.

After that episode, I learned what to do the next time. If you ever get stung, look for the tall, hairy, yellow-flowered mullein to crush and rub on the sting. Mullein is a popular folk antidote for bee stings, which also contain formic acid. Or soothe the sting with aloe vera. Or use a paste of meat tenderizer and water. The most recent thing I've read prescribed vitamin C in water applied directly to bites and stings. Although it may not work for nettles, it is miraculous on scalds. Crush a 1,000-milligram ascorbic acid pill with a hammer in a plastic bag, stir it until it's dissolved into ½ cup water, and apply the liquid directly to burns. It stops pain instantly, and there is no blistering or scarring.

Gather, wash, and steam a large bunch of nettles. Drain well. Make a medium or heavy cream sauce (see pages 183–84), and season it with onion and grated nutmeg. Mix it with the hot greens, and serve as a first course.

▦ WATERCRESS

Watercress *(Nasturtium officinale)* is one of our most popular wild greens. The name of the genus comes from *nasus,* "nose," and *torqus,* "twist." It seems to be a comic description of what one does when confronted with the smell of nasturtiums. The species name, *officinale,* always designates a plant that was once thought to be medically useful, or "officially" recognized.

DESCRIPTION, HABITAT, AND SEASON

Watercress is a succulent perennial with round compound leaves and tiny white flowers that grows in running water: creeks and rivers, stream-fed ponds, brooks, and even ditches, throughout the country. Watercress is tenderest and most flavorful in early spring, but available in all but the coldest weather. In the summer, its stems get leggy and its leaves get hot, but it may prevail in streams in autumn, and sometimes (though of course more rarely) throughout the winter—at least in the mid-Atlantic states. There are several varieties, some emerald green, and some with a dark red tinge to both the stems and leaves.

Watercress is antiscorbutic, diuretic, and has a good dose of several vital minerals including potassium, calcium, and iron. It is edible year-round, and even if it grows in a stream flowing through pastures used by cows and deer, bears and raccoons, it is safe to eat if you take precautions I'll describe later (see "Cleaning Watercress").

HISTORY AND LORE

The Romans fed watercress to the mentally ill as a cure. It is interesting that what the Romans may have noted is that people who are well nourished are healthier mentally as well as physically. Hildegard von Bingen, a twelfth-century mystic, wrote that anyone with jaundice or fever should steam watercress in a bowl, eat it warm, and drink the water. Its energy, she claimed, comes from water, so she believed watercress tea was a good food for someone so sick he could take only liquids. Indians used it as a treatment for kidney disorders, and as a cure for constipation. Early African-Americans used watercress as an abortifacient, and it was also believed to cause temporary sterility. On the other hand, watercress had among the Indians and early settlers a reputation as an aphrodisiac. Again, it is only speculation, but the high iodine content may help stimulate the thyroid gland, which, if underactive, leaves one generally sluggish.

R E C I P E S

Cleaning Watercress

Cut watercress stems just above the waterline. I use a sharp, long knife to skim along under the leaves at water level. This helps keep mud out of your takings. Once home, wash the leaves carefully in a large sinkful of cold water. Drain that off, run another sinkful, adding about $\frac{1}{4}$ cup chlorine bleach to that sinkful (or about 1 Tbsp. per gallon). Stir to mix the bleach in the water, then put the cress in it, dunk it under, and let it sit for 5 minutes. This will kill anything undesirable on the cress. Rinse 2 or 3 times to take away all traces of the disinfectant, and you'll have the best salad green you'll ever taste, the most delicate soup green. The several rinsings also assure that the cress (or other greens) will be clear of dirt. Nothing ruins a salad like grit.

Spring Salad

Anytime from early spring until hot weather, collect any tender greens, such as watercress, mustard, chicory, or dandelion. Add violet leaves and/or violet flowers. (Nasturtium flowers and leaves, close kin to watercress, are also delicious; see pages 125–26.) Remove any tough stems, and tear into bite-size pieces. Wash the greens very carefully. Salad ingredients can vary endlessly, according to what's available, and what you like. A spring salad with wild greens is not only delicious, but worth a hundred vitamin pills. You can also blend wild greens with the more familiar romaine, endive, butter, or Boston lettuce, red lettuce, radicchio, and so on. Search creatively at any grocery store as well as in the fields. Most greens other than lettuce have more food value than lettuce, as well as more taste. Many vegetables sold as pot greens are also good in salads, such as mustard, kale, and chard. Dress lightly with Salad Dressing (see recipe, pages 176–77).

Watercress Bisque
(Serves four to five.)

This is popular in upscale restaurants both here and in continental Europe. The less you cook the watercress, the better the soup will be. Chop a big bunch of washed watercress coarsely, and set aside. Sauté 1 small chopped onion in 2 Tbsp. butter until soft. Stir in 2 Tbsp. flour to make a roux. Stir for 2 minutes over medium heat, but do not let the roux brown. Slowly add about 1 quart chicken or beef broth (see recipes, pages 175–76). Reserve 1 cup of the watercress for garnish. Add the rest of the watercress and cook 1 minute. Add one of the following to the soup: a 3-oz. block of cream cheese, warmed to room temperature; or 1 cup cream; or 1 cup sour cream. When the mixture just begins to boil, take it off the heat, stir in the reserved, uncooked cress, and serve the soup at once.

Watercress Sandwiches

Collect a bunch of watercress about the size of a basketball, or gather a gallon-size plastic bag full. Wash the cress well, strip off the leaves from the tough center stems, and chop it up fairly well. By then you'll have about 1 quart. Cream a large package of cream cheese (you can use Neufchâtel or fat-free) with 2 Tbsp. good mayonnaise *or* butter. To this mixture add 1 small crushed clove garlic and about 1 Tbsp. shaved onion. A little grated cucumber is good, too. Add the chopped watercress and beat until blended. Add pepper to taste. Stand a loaf of soft white sandwich bread upright on the counter, out of its wrap, and gently shave off the crusts on all sides with a serrated knife, sawing slowly down from top to bottom. Then, smear each square with some of the mixture, and gently roll each into a cylinder. Pack them close together to prevent unrolling, or secure each with a tooth-pick. Or just make crustless tea sandwiches, and slice them crosswise into triangles. Cover the sandwiches with a soaked and wrung-out clean cloth and refrigerate until serving time. If possible, arrange on a bed of more fresh dewy watercress (or other greens) to serve. As everyone knows, these are the epitome of elegance for English teas and lawn parties.

Mustard or land cress leaves substituted in this recipe also make great sandwiches.

If you don't have mayonnaise on hand, see page 176 for how to make it yourself.

◼ WILD ONIONS AND GARLIC

The *Allium* (Latin for "garlic") genus is a large one, and includes at least a dozen pungent herbs of the Northern Hemisphere. All are oniony or garlicky in odor and flavor. *Allium canadense, A. sativum,* and *A. vineale* are some of the most common wild garlics that grow throughout Canada, and pretty much all over the forty-eight states below. *A. cernuum, A. stellatum,* and *A. textile* are common onions. *A. tricoccum* is the wild leek, or ramp; it is ubiquitous

Wild Garlic

throughout the United States and Canada, though most celebrated in West Virginia. *A. schoenoprasum* is the wild chive. Use them interchangeably.

Description, Habitat, and Season

Onions and garlic, chives and leeks, all grow from base bulbs, and bear flowers of purple or white on a leafless stalk that often turns into a little bulb itself. All have green stalks, either flat like onion leaves or round and hollow like chive or scallion leaves, above bulbs that smell distinctly oniony or garlicky. But beware: Onion and garlic belong to the lily family, and some similar-looking (but not similar-smelling) flat-leaved, bulbous plants can be poisonous. A case in point is lily of the valley (which can look at lot like ramp). If a bulbed plant looking like a wild onion does not immediately smell garlicky or oniony, let it alone.

In Virginia, there is not a month of the year that some wild onion or garlic can't be found, though some species are early, some late, and they are certainly more common in spring. They flourish in woods, lawns, gardens, parks, in sun or shade. In the wild I find it sometimes difficult to distinguish between the two odors (so that I'm not sure if I have onion or garlic). But never mind; they are all good to eat, bulb and stalks, though you may find that some are too tough to use.

History and Lore

In times when plague rampaged throughout cities in Europe, a garlic clove carried in the mouth was believed to protect the user. Garlic was supposed to be effective against vampires, too. One wonders if it was that garlic so isolated the taker that no one, vampire or otherwise, would come near.

West Virginia has made famous *A. tricoccum,* the ramp or wild leek, and sponsors a spring ramp festival when these flat-leaved, light green onions are ready to eat. Folklore has it that a ramp eater can coexist only with another ramp eater for several days after eating the plants, until the body has rid itself of the sulfur compounds caused by eating the strong-flavored plant. But I have eaten ramps on many occasions when people I live with have not, and nobody has shunned me. In my opinion, ramps do you no more harm, fragrantly speaking, than garlic does.

When I was a kid, spring milk tasted of onion and garlic when the cows ate them along with the new grass in the fields. Nowadays, I learn, the reason we don't have oniony milk in the spring is that dairy farmers don't graze cattle the way they used to, but rather give them prepackaged feed. Even those farmers who graze their cows on fresh grass make sure in the spring (when there might be wild onions in the grass) that the cows are not let out of the barns until they are full, so that they are unlikely to munch onions, or even grass. They just want to lie down and chew their cud.

Garlic and onion are both mildly antiseptic, and in recent years garlic has been raised from obnoxious insignificance to a place of honor: Both onions and garlic appear from some clinical studies to be effective in lowering cholesterol, as a first-line defense against colds, and even might be useful in preventing cancer.

R E C I P E S

Ramps with Eggs

Carefully clean a mess of ramps or any wild onions, removing the roots, and chopping the bulbs and stems coarsely. Melt a small amount of butter, oil, margarine, or bacon grease in a frying pan, and cook the ramps covered until limp and beginning to brown. Beat some eggs with milk or cream, and a little salt. Pour the eggs over the ramps and scramble quickly, not overcooking. This is a typical ramp dish, though ramps are also eaten fried, and made into ramp pies, or quiches.

Onions with Pasta
(Serves four to six.)

When you put the water on to boil for the pasta, melt a stick of unsalted butter, and sauté as many (up to a whole gallon-size plastic bag full) wild onions, garlic, or ramps as you want, tops and bulbs together. Sprinkle with 2 tsp. sugar, reduce heat, and cook slowly for ½ hour, which allows the sugar to begin to caramelize, and the butter taste to thoroughly permeate the onions. Cook 1 lb. of pasta al dente. When the pasta is ready, add ½ cup white wine or dry sherry to the onions, stir in and cook for just 1 or 2 minutes, and toss with the freshly cooked pasta. Taste, then salt and pepper lightly if needed. Serve with freshly grated Parmesan, pecorino, or Romano cheese for a meal of great delicacy. Note: Olive oil might be substituted in this recipe, but it will taste quite different. The slow cooking and caramelizing in the butter give this dish its unusual taste. Red onions or yellow may also be substituted if you haven't got any wild onions.

FUNGI: MUSHROOMS

. . . it is not those far-fetched fruits which the speculator imports that concern us chiefly, but rather those which you have fetched yourself in the hold of a basket, from some far hill or swamp, journeying all the long afternoon, the first of the season, consigned to your friends at home.

—Henry David Thoreau

Mushrooms are among the most mysterious plants on earth. The word *mushroom* is thought to derive from an Old French word, *mousseron,* meaning "moss grower." They spring up apparently out of nowhere overnight, and disappear nearly as quickly. Their growth habits were not well understood until recently. Some gleam at night with a green phosphorescence. Many fungi grow in ever-widening circles. Some toxic mushrooms have long been part of certain secret rituals, providing mind-altering substances. Thus mushrooms have been revered as doorways to other dimensions that only the users are privileged to visit.

One theologian, John Allegro, in *The Sacred Mushroom and the Cross*, states that the Egyptian mushroom hieroglyph, long believed to represent a kind of parasol, really represents the toxic *Amanita muscaria* mushroom, which in its early stages of poisoning causes bright hallucinations. The mushroom is phallic in appearance, and is "born" from a volva that looks like an egg. Allegro thinks that there has existed throughout the ages a mushroom cult—and that the Christ figure actually evolved from this primitive fertility cult.

The word *toadstool*, though colorfully evocative, refers usually to any mushroom that is poisonous. To forage for mushrooms you will need good mushroom field guides. Choose one with drawings or tinted lithographs, and another with good photographs of the mushrooms, for there *are* poisonous mushrooms that can kill you. But my philosophy about that is similar to my philosophy about poisonous snakes and Lyme ticks: You don't stay out of the woods because there are things in there that might hurt you; you just proceed with caution and awareness. In the case of fungi, stay with the safe ones.

Fungi like wet weather, wet wood, wet woods. They are plants lacking chlorophyll, which is the green-making chemical of most plants, and they flourish in heat and dampness. There are thousands of different kinds of mushrooms, and thousands more fungi, a huge group without which we could not live, including everything from the yeast that raises our bread to the beast that gives you athlete's foot.

If you want to test mushrooms for safety that are not described herein, a step further is to make a spore print, a simple process that I often use to identify new fungi. All you need is a pack of black construction paper, and regular white paper. To make a spore print, lay a piece of black paper slightly overlapping a white one. Then lay an open mushroom, gills down, over the line where the black paper and the white paper meet, so that its spores will fall half on white paper, and half on black. Cover the mushroom with an upside-down bowl, and leave it for two to eight hours. Then examine the spores. Compare them with what your books say; all mushroom books identify the color of the spore print. The spores will deposit on the two colors of paper, and the contrast will allow you to see the subtlety of the spore color.

A flat-bottomed basket for gathering keeps the mushrooms in good shape, though a grocery bag or plastic bag will do. You can pretty much tell from your specimens which ones need special pampering, and which are all right to toss into a plastic sack.

Mushrooms sometimes get a bad rap because of the harmful varieties. But good mushrooms, if you stay with those easy to identify, are nearly calorie-free, taste like the woodland air smells after rain, are easy to find, and make delicious meatless gourmet dishes. In all the mushroom recipes, any mushroom can really be substituted for any other. And once again, amounts of the mushroom are not crucial.

> Mushrooms (and eggplant) are the worst culprits for soaking up oil and butter. Try brushing them lightly with oil or melted butter and roasting them in the oven for the same effect.

I offer here only easily identifiable fungi. For heaven's sake, never taste a mushroom you can't identify. *Do not try to identify any mushroom by my description only.* You need to check with at least one other reference, and possibly a third. The best guides, in my estimation, are Alexander H. Smith's *The Mushroom Hunter's Field Guide, Revised and Enlarged,* U. Michigan, 1966; and Orson K. Miller's *Mushrooms of North America,* Dutton.

▣ MORELS

Morels *(Morchella appalachiensis, M. esculenta, M. angusticeps, M. deliciosa, M. crassipes)* are possibly the most delicious wild mushrooms, and once identified, impossible to confuse with any others. *Morchella* is simply the Latin term for "mushroom," and *esculenta* and *deliciosa* mean that one is "edible" and the other "delicious." *Angusticeps* means "narrow," and *appalachiensis* is the name of the subspecies that grows in the Appalachian Mountains from Newfoundland to Georgia; mycologists differ on whether it is a different subspecies from *angusticeps*. Morels, popular throughout the Temperate Zone here and in Europe, go by various folk names. They are called land fish or upland fish (perhaps from their shape, perhaps from their elusive flavor, which I would call earthy but which some might call fishy); marls (surely a corruption of the name, but also maybe after the kind of soft, crumbly rock geologists call marl, which is full of holes and pits like the fungi); merkles, which some think is a corruption of *miracles*; smokies (the dark ones); honeycomb mushrooms; sponge mushrooms; musharoons, which one assumes comes from a folksy mishearing; and morchellas, from the Latin name. There is a dark morel, ranging in color from gray to tan to rusty brown, a pale golden one, and a grayish white one. All are fine to eat.

DESCRIPTION, HABITAT, AND SEASON

Though the dark ones *(M. angusticeps* and *M. appalachiensis)* appear a couple of weeks earlier than the lighter ones, they overlap, and most "messes" will have specimens of two or three kinds, including one that may or may not be a true morel, but looks like the others, *M. semilibra,* or the half-free morel (so called because the cap attaches to the stalk halfway down the cap). It is also edible. Morels pop up in hardwood forests in the middle of spring "when the oak leaves are the size of mouse ears," and are said to be especially numerous in years and places following a forest fire. Where you find jack-in-the-pulpits and trillium, look for morels. Some variety grows everywhere north of the Tropics all the way to the Arctic Circle.

All morels have the characteristic appearance variously described as pitted, ridged, spongelike, cone shaped, wrinkled; all are between three and six inches high; all have hollow stems and hollow interiors;

and all are shaped vaguely like trees. They have no gills. None of them is easy to see on the woodland floor. The flavor is absolutely gorgeous: smoky, earthy, elusive.

A flat basket is probably the best thing to take picking, for it keeps the delicate morels intact better than the grocery bags or plastic bags. But a flat basket is unwieldy, and I opt rather for the convenience of a red plastic tote. (Red can be seen from a distance, and you can use it to mark a hunting boundary while you are circling looking for mushrooms.)

HISTORY AND LORE

Morels are so wonderful that even poets have eulogized them. Among the best descriptions is that of my friend, the poet William Jay Smith:

Not ringed but rare, not gilled but polyp-like, having
sprung up overnight—

These mushrooms of the gods, resembling human organs
uprooted, rooted only on the air,

Looking like lungs wrenched from the human body, lungs
reversed, not breathing internally

But being the externalization of breath itself, these
spicy, twisted cones,

These perforated brown-white asparagus tips—these morels,
smelling of wet graham crackers mixed with maple leaves;

. . . Tasting of the sweet damp woods and of the rain one inch
above the meadow:

It was like feasting upon air.

R E C I P E S

As morels are hollow, they need special cleaning treatment. Slice each in half from top to bottom to determine if it houses any insalubrious creatures: I've found stones, centipedes, and slugs inside morels, so be warned. Then jostle them in warm, heavily salted water for about 5 minutes (this dislodges any dirt fragments that may be caught in the wrinkled surface) before draining the halves on paper towels. The salt will force out the tiny wood fleas that also call these mushrooms home.

There are several ways to keep morels. Of course they are best used fresh, as most things are. But once cooked, they can be frozen. Some folks dry morels by sewing them onto a string and putting them in a warm, dry oven or attic until they are totally dry, or using a dehydrator.

Morels and Wild Rice Casserole
(For a crowd, to celebrate spring.)

Preheat the oven to 350°F. Assemble a basketful of morels, butter, onion, celery, wild rice, 2 cups chicken or beef broth, 1 can smoked almonds, white rice, dry sherry, and fresh parsley.

Sauté at least 2 dozen morels in a little or a lot of butter, stirring occasionally, for 5 to 10 minutes. Set aside. In 4 Tbsp. butter sauté 1 cup chopped onion and a few finely chopped center stalks of celery, with leaves (about 1 cup). Add to this 1 cup washed, uncooked wild rice, and 2 cups salted chicken or beef broth. Cover and simmer on low heat for 35 minutes. While the rice is simmering, chop the cup of almonds. Set them aside.

To the half-cooked wild rice, add 1 cup plain uncooked rice and 1 cup each salted water or water with a bouillon cube dissolved in it, and dry sherry. Stir, turn the rice immediately into a greased casserole, add the morels and almonds, stir again, and bake covered in the oven for about 1 hour, or until the liquid is all absorbed. You may want to sprinkle chopped parsley on the finished product. You can leave out the almonds, or substitute roasted pecans. The best accompaniment for this is briefly steamed, fresh wild asparagus.

Morel or Other Mushroom Soufflé
(Serves four.)

Chop 20 to 30 morels finely, and sauté them in 2 Tbsp. butter, margarine, or bacon fat. For this recipe, olive oil isn't recommended. Sprinkle them with 1 Tbsp. flour, stir over heat to make a roux, add about 2 Tbsp. heavy cream, stir until thick, and dust with nutmeg. This will make about 1 cup. Cool slightly.

After, follow the Soufflé instructions (see pages 177–78) using a straight-sided soufflé dish, 5 eggs plus 1 extra egg white. Don't forget to preheat your oven. Beat the yolks until smooth. Beat the whites until glossy, add a little of the mushroom mix to the yolks, then add the yolks back into the mushroom mix. Add a big spoonful of the whites to "lighten" the mushrooms, then fold it all into the rest of the whites carefully. Bake until the center is just firm, and serve at once.

▣ PUFFBALLS

Puffball, like so many folk names for plants, describes this fungus well: a puffy ball. This fungus belongs to several related species. Its most common genus name, *Calvatia*, comes from the Latin word *calva*, meaning "scalp," "bald head," or even "skull," which aptly describes this round, whitish fungus. The western puffball, *Calbovista subsculpta*, has *bovis* in the name, perhaps suggesting its propensity to grow in cow fields; *subsculpta* describes the peculiar carved effect of the surface.

DESCRIPTION, HABITAT, AND SEASON

Puffballs grow all over the world in Temperate Zones, in the spring or in wet summer weather, but most often they pop up overnight in the

Chicory turning blue to pink.

Dandelions can be found almost anywhere.

A beautiful bunch of fresh asparagus.

Cinnamon fern fiddleheads.

Land cress can be found year-round.

Katie Letcher Lyle

Katie Letcher Lyle

Land cress on the left and wild mustard on the right.

Lamb's-quarters growing by a fencepost.

Katie Letcher Lyle

Katie Letcher Lyle

Milkweed is a delicious early summer green.

Wild mustard can spice up any salad.

Katie Letcher Lyle

Katie Letcher Lyle

Wild onion in winter.

Katie Letcher Lyle

A large cluster of stinging nettles.

Sorrel in bloom.

Watercress in winter.

Pokeberries are toxic — use only the young greens.

Blueberries.

Elderberries.

Huckleberries in bloom.

Katie Letcher Lyle

A good-sized puffball.

Katie Letcher Lyle

A single morel peeking up from the forest floor.

Katie Letcher Lyle

A batch of mixed morels, cut length-wise and washed.

Katie Letcher Lyle

Chanterelles are great sautéed in butter.

A sizable outcropping of sulpher shelf mushrooms.

Michael & Linda Hoffman, Honey Hollow Farm, Middleburgh, NY

The inky cap of a coprinus mushroom.

Katie Letcher Lyle

Katie Letcher Lyle

Oyster mushrooms favor older trees.

Katie Letcher Lyle

Boletes, or porcini mushrooms, dry very well.

Katie Letcher Lyle

Field mushrooms come in a variety of sizes.

Lilly Golden

Wild apples bear little resemblance to those
you find in stores, but they taste just as good.

Crab apples make great jelly.

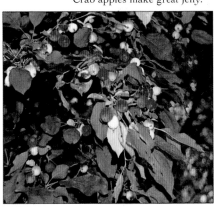

Katie Letcher Lyle

Blackberries ripening in the wild.

Katie Letcher Lyle

A raspberry blossom in spring.

A sea of cranberries afloat in a bog in Nantucket.

A wild cherry tree can offer an abundance of cherries.

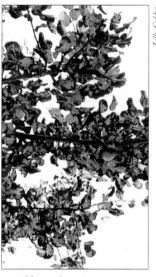

A wild pear hanging just out of reach.

Wild grapes range in size and color—but all are good to eat.

Fig trees are small and shrub-like, and found only in the southern United States.

Beach plums.

A quince flower in bloom.

Quince are best harvested after they ripen and make a wonderful tart jelly.

Violets in full bloom.

A wild strawberry blossom.

Jerusalem artichokes are wildflowers related to the sunflower.

Rosehips, the fruit of both
wild and tame rose bushes,
are rich in vitamin C.

You will usually smell a wild mint patch before you see it.

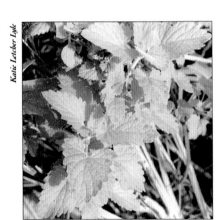

Catnip makes a great tea in addition to amusing the family cat.

The bright orange flower of the nasturtium is hard to miss.

Marigolds are beautiful in the garden and delicious in tea.

Black walnuts are found with
a greenish husk over the shell.

A butternut tree.

A shagbark hickory tree.

Beechnuts.

Pecan nuts still on the tree.

Horseradish root can be jarred and stored.

A small sassafras plant.

Horseradish is a leafy green best collected in the spring.

Unless you are adept at climbing trees, coconuts are best gathered once they have fallen to the ground.

Ginseng leaves and berries help to identify the plant, but have no other uses.

A pile of ginseng roots ready to be dried.

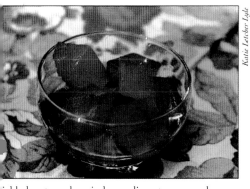

ickled watermelon rind compliments any meal.

Avocados still on the tree are not ripe yet.

Both the pads and fruit of the prickly pear cactus are good to eat.

The bright yellow flowers of the prickly pear in bloom.

Wild rice growing in a field.

Sugar maples are the source of sweet maple syrup, shown here jarred and ready to serve.

early fall, after rain, in fields. They like golf courses, lawns, and pastures, and return to the same locale year after year. Puffballs vary enormously in size, at their smallest like round white golf balls, and at their largest like round lightly browned loaves of bread six to eight inches across. They are pure white throughout, with no gill structure, and are firm and foamlike inside, something like dense angel food cake in both weight and consistency. A western species has flattish, conelike scales covering the surface. Throw out any that are not pure white throughout, or that smell like wet dog, have soft spots, worm holes, or insects in them.

Puffballs can be safely collected in baskets or bags. Once home, they need a quick rinse to get any dirt off the outer surfaces. Always slice small puffballs through from top to bottom to make sure they are white throughout. Since *Amanita,* deadly poisonous white-gilled mushrooms, do often grow among other mushrooms, be sure you haven't accidentally picked up the button form of an *Amanita.* If you have, you will clearly see the outline of the gill structure, stalk, veil, and cap. Of course you must discard that specimen, and wash your knife well before going on to the next mushroom.

R E C I P E S

If the mushrooms are a firm, solid white "sponge" throughout, then they can be sliced, diced, or chopped, and sautéed slowly, or sliced and brushed with oil or melted butter and baked until brown. They can be frozen after cooking for later use if there are too many to eat right away. I have never heard of anyone trying to dry puffballs, though in theory it ought to be possible, if you slice them thin.

Puffball Slices Sauté

Cut the puffballs in $\frac{3}{4}$-inch slices, and sauté them in pure butter, or 1 Tbsp. butter and 1 Tbsp. salad oil, until nicely browned. Sprinkle lightly with lemon juice and salt for a wonderful side dish.

▣ CHANTERELLES

Chanterelles *(Cantharellus cibarius)* are midsummer wet-weather mushrooms that can be seen from afar. The Latin name of the genus, *Cantharellus,* comes from *cantharus,* "a drinking goblet," and thus defines the shape perfectly. The black chanterelle is indeed reminiscent in shape of a cornucopia, whose name derives from the word for horn in Latin. All are wonderful.

DESCRIPTION, HABITAT, AND SEASON

Chanterelles have fluted edges, are shaped like flared wineglasses or vases, and in place of gills underneath they have veins. Chanterelles come in many colors. The easiest to see, *C. cibarius,* are egg-yolk yellow, and look like flowers blooming on the forest floor. There are also white chanterelles in New England woods called *C. subalbidus,* or "almost white," and black or gray chanterelles called *Craterellus cornucopioides,* which describes the fungi as both "crated" and "cornucopia shaped." These are called also death trumpets, though they are delicious and safe. There is a gray-purple-brown chanterelle called *Cantharellus clavatus* (which means club shaped, from the Latin *clavus*), and tiny red-orange, or cinnabar, chanterelles called *Cantharellus cinnabarinus.* These mushrooms, like most others, spread by underground mycelia (tiny white threads you sometimes see hanging off the bottoms), so look year after year in the same locality where you found them once. I have found chanterelles most often in coniferous, especially pine, woods, a day to three days after a good soaking rain in midsummer.

As usual, a basket with a wide bottom would be best, but a flat-bottomed bag, or even a plastic bag, will do.

R E C I P E S

Collect only the young mushrooms. Insects also find chanterelles delicious, and since you don't want to ruin your batch with one bug-infested specimen, check for insect infestation by cutting the stem off halfway between the veins and the soil, and checking the stem. If it has bug tunnels, discard the specimen.

Stewed Chanterelles
(For pasta, rice, steak, or toast.)

Melt a small amount of butter over medium-low heat, add clean chanterelles, sliced if they are big, and sauté, stirring occasionally to coat mushrooms evenly. Add a splash of dry wine, cover, stew for about 20 minutes, and salt lightly. Chanterelles need slow, relatively long cooking, as they can be tough. Add a squeeze of lemon juice, and serve them at once on pasta, rice or wild rice, steak or roast beef, or toast.

▧ SULFUR SHELF

The name *Polyporus sulphureus* tells anyone with even a smattering of Latin that this is a many-pored mushroom of a yellow hue. The common name sulfur shelf mushroom describes its growth pattern, out from the trunk of a tree like a pile of shelves, as well as its sulfur yellow color. This is sometimes called the chicken mushroom: The flesh is fairly dry, dense, and tastes much like chicken breast.

DESCRIPTION, HABITAT, AND SEASON

Polyporus sulphureus are easy to identify: They grow in midsummer on the sides of hardwood trees, or on rotting logs, are sunset orange colored on top, with fluted edges, and yellow, porous bottoms instead of gills. Sulfur shelf fungi sometimes grow to enormous size, with brackets climbing many feet up on a tree. However, if the ones you find are big, take only the smallest, freshest brackets, or the outer edges, for the older part closer to the tree can be tough and strong-flavored, not to mention full of bugs. These fungi aren't as fragile as most, so they needn't be treated with as much delicacy. Merely take them home, carefully brush and rinse off all dirt, and drain until dry on paper towels.

R E C I P E S

Sulfur shelf mushrooms are best, I think, creamed. They need thin slicing and slow cooking or sautéing, as they are tougher than most mushrooms. But they have a wonderful flavor.

Creamed Sulfur Shelf

Slice about 1 quart sulfur shelf fungi thinly, and sauté in butter and a bit of mashed garlic for 10 minutes. Make a cream sauce (see pages 183–84) using 2 Tbsp. flour, 2 Tbsp. butter, and 2 Tbsp. cream, and enough dry sherry or milk (or a combination) for the consistency you like. Add salt and pepper to taste. These are great served on toast, rice, pasta, or alone.

Funghi Italiano

Slice the sulfur shelf mushrooms thinly, and sauté in olive oil, not too much, with chopped garlic added. Stir frequently, salt and pepper to taste, finish with fresh lemon juice sprinkled over the whole, and stir one last time. Sprinkle with chopped parsley before serving. Serve alone or tossed with hot pasta.

▣ OYSTER MUSHROOMS

The botanical name of this mushroom, *Pleurotus ostreatus* or *P. sapidus,* comes from the word for the lining of the thorax that covers the lungs, *pleura,* and is kin to our word for the inflammation of that lining, *pleurisy.* It is likely that the shape of the mushroom suggested this name. *Ostreatus* is Latin for "oyster," and *sapidus* means "flavorful," or "sapid."

DESCRIPTION, HABITAT, AND SEASON

Oyster mushrooms grow from spring to fall on the sides of dying hardwood trees or from the tops or sides of dead stumps, and are creamy and grayish in color, or even lavender-white. They are rounded down at the margins, with off-center thick, tough stalks and white gills, caps of unequal size, and a delicate odor like oysters. *Pleurotus* are now often available in grocery stores.

R E C I P E S

When you find oyster mushrooms, slice off only the fresh ends of the mushroom tops, or the small young growth. The old part closest to the stalks may be tough. *Pleurotus* need scrupulous cleaning to remove the little hard, black beetles that like to live in the gills. Soak them in warm salted water for a few minutes, jostle them up and down in the water, and drain and pat them dry before using. Sliced, sautéed, and made into soup or a casserole, they are especially wonderful, and taste much like scalloped oysters.

Faux Oyster Stew

For this elegant soup, you might want to keep the mushrooms as whole as possible (to be suggestive of the shapes of oysters), though you can also slice or chop them.

Sauté in a large saucepan with about 4 Tbsp. butter 25 to 50 oyster mushrooms (and a bit of diced onion and celery if you like). As they begin to brown a bit, add a splash of dry sherry. Cover and cook 5 minutes. Sprinkle with 4 Tbsp. flour and a half of a nutmeg, grated, and stir until smooth. Slowly add 1 quart milk, and a little salt and pepper, stirring constantly. Simmer gently just until bubbles begin to form around the edge of the pan. Take the soup off the heat before it boils, and serve at once. You can also use half chicken broth and half cream, or milk and half and half, or even evaporated skim milk. (The process for this rich soup works equally well with any mushroom.)

▣ BOLETUS

Boletes *(Boletus castaneus)* are great favorites in Europe, and gaining popularity in America. In Italy these beloved fungi are called *porcini* ("pig food"), in France, *cepes* (this word derives from an old French word for onion, *caepa*), and in Germany, *Steinpilz,* or "stone mushrooms." (They may in fact appear from a distance like stones.) The genus name *Boletus* comes from *bolo,* the word for "ball," and the species name, *castaneus,* Latin for "chestnut," probably refers to their toasty brown color. They are also called *B. edulis,* the "edible boletus."

DESCRIPTION, HABITAT, AND SEASON

Boletes are large autumn mushrooms, three inches to a foot across, and grow in coniferous forests in America and Europe. They have brown, dry, rounded tops with creamy pores underneath instead of gills, and fat reticulated (crisscrossed like netting) stalks. Having tested probably two dozen different boletes, the chestnut, or edible, boletus is the only one I would recommend. Some are poisonous: Avoid any that are red, or that stain blue when a piece of the flesh is broken off. The American chestnut boletus has a look-alike that is benign, but bitter tasting. The ones you want are toasty brown, have firm ivory flesh, a mild earthy odor, and a pleasant taste.

HISTORY AND LORE

Boletes are marvelous, and safe if you identify them carefully. They apparently dry well, and that is how they are sold in Italy, though the ones I've tried to dry in Virginia have molded before I could dry them out.

Boletes are the "toadstools" you frequently see in illustrations for fairy tales; elves are rumored to use the big boleti for resting places.

R E C I P E S

Porcini in Puff Pastry
(Serves four to six.)

Preheat the oven to 400°F. Thaw 1 sheet of commercial puff pastry for 20 minutes, and roll it into a 12" × 14" rectangle. Sauté 1 cup or so sliced boletus (or other) mushrooms in 2 Tbsp. butter and 1 or 2 crushed or minced cloves garlic, and season to taste with salt, pepper, a squeeze of lemon juice, and a scattering of nutmeg. Sprinkle the lightly browned fungi with 2 Tbsp. flour, and stir until a roux is formed. Add 2 to 4 Tbsp.

> I sauté all my wild mushrooms in a little butter, and freeze them for further use in labeled Ziploc sandwich bags. The cooking stops the natural enzyme action that causes them to spoil, as well as reducing them in volume.

heavy cream to the mix, stirring well. The sauce should be thick. Spoon the mix down the center of the rolled-out dough, fold both sides over the middle, and press a fork along both ends to seal the puff. Quickly brush the top with cream before putting it in the oven, to enhance browning. Bake 15 to 20 minutes, or until puffed and golden. Let cool about 10 minutes. Slice for a sublime first course.

Grilled Porcini
(Serves four.)

Slice 2 large boletus (or 4 smaller specimens) thickly. Brush them with 2 Tbsp. melted butter and 2 Tbsp. olive oil with a mashed clove of garlic added. Salt them lightly, and lay them on a hot grill. Turn them after 5 minutes, and sprinkle them with ½ cup hearty dry red wine, such as Chianti, watch them carefully, and cook 5 more minutes. Remove to a plate and keep warm. Arrange slices on four plates with parsley garnishes for a delicate first course. Serve with crusty Italian bread. This recipe also works well with the large Portobello mushrooms now available in stores.

▨ COPRINUS

Coprinus atramentarius, and *C. micaceus*, both called inky caps, are humble in the world of fungi. Their genus name comes from the Greek word kopros, meaning "excrement." They often grow where there is deadwood, or in fields frequented by cows. The *C. micaceus* has granules much like the tops of sugar cookies (*mica* in Latin is "crumb" or "grain"), while *C. atramentarius* (meaning only "edible") does not; otherwise they are similar.

The largest of this autodigestive genus, *C. comatus*, the shaggy-mane mushroom, has scales that become curly or shaggy, and gills that become inky with age. *Coma* is the Latin word for "hair." Shaggymanes can be found along paved roadways, driveways, and sidewalks, as well as in fields and lawns.

Description, Habitat, and Season

The coprini are bell-shaped mushrooms usually on thin, brittle stalks, most often found in urban settings, especially around the stumps or bases of old rotting trees, and sometimes they are as dense as a carpet. You can find them in spring, summer, and autumn, in muggy weather after rain. They are grayish brown, deeply striated, packed together, and distinguishable because they are autodigestive. That means that the older specimens have a wet, black, melted appearance at the margins, caused by the process of self-digestion. They range in size from under an inch to nearly two inches in diameter.

Coprini may be ignored by some, because many of them are small, and difficult to clean: They push dirt up with them, on top of them, and are packed so densely that it's sometimes hard to get them to part company with their clods of dirt. They are also thin fleshed, and break easily. But all the coprini are absolutely delicious, and to my mind, worth the trouble. Also, you don't have to go far to find them. They probably grow somewhere on your street, or in your yard, or near your woodpile. They love the mulched ground underneath our azaleas. I've seen them come up through concrete driveways and, once, beside a bathroom toilet, during a rainy summer.

R E C I P E S

Sautéed Coprini
(For rice, pizza, or pasta.)

Wash coprini carefully, discarding any old, deteriorating specimens. Drain them thoroughly on plenty of paper towels or Turkish towels. Melt 3 or 4 Tbsp. butter or olive oil over medium heat, and add the drained mushrooms. Season with a little salt and pepper, some garlic if you like, a squeeze of lemon juice. Being thin fleshed, the coprini cook down quickly and release a dark, rich gravy. At this point, you may dry them out by keeping them over the heat until the liquid is evaporated, and use them to scatter on pizza. Or you may add a little cream to the mushrooms before they dry out, and serve them on rice or pasta.

Mushroom Pizza

Make a pizza crust according to the process in the appendix (see pages 178–80). Lightly oil the pizza by drizzling with 1 tsp. olive oil. Scatter the top with sliced fresh coprinus, morel, or field mushrooms sautéed lightly in olive oil. Sprinkle with chopped garlic, salt, pepper, parsley, a bit of fresh basil. Add a light layer of grated Parmesan cheese, and bake quickly (about 10 minutes) until it begins to brown, for the best pizza you ever tasted.

▦ FIELD MUSHROOMS

The field mushroom, *Agaricus campestris,* is America's most popular mushroom. Its close relative, *A. bisporus,* or the double-spored *Agaricus,* is the button mushroom available fresh in grocery stores, the mushroom found in commercially canned mushroom soup. They are the fungi most widely used in America, and called, simply, mushrooms. *Agaricus* comes from a word in Latin, *ager,* related to acre and agriculture, meaning "productive field" or "pasture." *Campestris* is related to campus in English, and in Latin it, too, means "plain," "open level spot," or "field." Both names tell clearly where this mushroom is to be found. The French name, *champignon (champs* plus *pignon),* means "field nut."

DESCRIPTION, HABITAT, AND SEASON

The favorite habitats of field mushrooms are golf courses, fields where cattle graze, parks, and wide lawns. They like wet weather and grow in late summer or early fall, sometimes in prodigious quantities, often in small or large circles, from white buttons about an inch in diameter to big specimens five inches across. Their color is whitish to pale beige. The way to identify them is to pick a young, an old, and an in-between specimen. The young buttons have tender, pale pink or flesh-colored gills, sometimes still folded into themselves; in time the young gills darken to a chocolaty brown, and the old, larger specimens have very dark reddish brown or blackish brown gills. *Avoid any field mushrooms with white gills.*

Take along a flat-bottomed basket to gather field mushrooms, for they are a bit brittle, and have a slight tendency to break. Also take along a knife, with which to cut the caps off just beneath the caps. This avoids most of the dirt that so often clings to the stems, which are stringy and tough anyway.

R E C I P E S

Try to brush the dirt off field mushrooms, then rinse them off with water instead of soaking them, for they blot up water like sponges and you might end up with a watery mess of spore-stained mushrooms. If you have to dunk them, then drain them thoroughly on paper towels or Turkish towels before you cook them.

In the early fall, field mushrooms are often so numerous you can gather a year's supply in an hour. After sautéing them in butter, you can freeze them in small containers for year-round use.

Mushroom-Stuffed Chicken with Gravy
(Serves two to four.)

Preheat the oven to 350°F. Wash a raw young frying chicken well, and rub it inside and outside with crushed garlic and salt. Stuff it full and overflowing with fresh, raw, salted field mushrooms or morels. Let them overflow the cavity and fall around the chicken. Bake the bird at 350°F for 1½ hours. Rice and gravy is the perfect accompaniment. Cook the rice on top of the stove. When the chicken is done, with a basting syringe, suck up about 1 cup of the cooking liquid, which will be dark, rich, and delicious. To a small pan, add 2 or 3 Tbsp. flour, then add the chicken-mushroom liquid slowly, stirring the whole time until you have an unbelievably delicious gravy. If it gets too thick, add a little water and keep stirring. Add 1 Tbsp. soy sauce at the end for the richest flavor. This will serve four in a pinch, or three, but it's delicious enough that two people can devour it with ease.

Mushroom Catsup

This condiment was more popular in England in the nineteenth century than tomato catsup, and reminds the taste buds of Worcestershire sauce, steak sauce, and catsup. If you get a bumper crop of field mushrooms and have extras, give this a try.

Mushrooms, once cleaned, can be cooked whole, chopped, or sliced. The best way is to cook them in a scant amount of butter, bacon fat, or vegetable oil brought to medium-high heat, the mushrooms stirred in quickly, and a top put on the pan. Cook only a few minutes. Mushrooms are about 99 percent water, so no extra is needed when you cook them. You can add a smashed clove of garlic to 1 stick butter, and use part of that for a bunch of mushrooms—but be careful not to use too much garlic. Or you can add a scant spoonful of bacon fat to a big pan of the fungi to enhance the natural smokiness. In my part of Appalachia, many folks cook morels in plain bacon grease, but that would overwhelm their delicate flavor, in my opinion. They can also be prepared by steaming for 1 or 2 minutes or with no more than 1 Tbsp. water. I've steamed them in ½ cup dry sherry, and that's better. One or 2 Tbsp. brandy might be sprinkled over a ready panful, lit, and the blue flame savored by the eye before the dish is savored on the tongue. But go easy; mostly you want to taste the mushrooms.

In an earthenware dish, pack freshly gathered and cleaned mushrooms in layers, with salt in between. Let sit covered for a day in a cool spot. Mash and strain through several layers of cheesecloth. To every quart liquid add 1 oz. peppercorns, a fat slice of ginger, 12 cloves, and 1 cracked nutmeg (or 3 blades mace). Boil gently for 15 minutes, and allow to cool. Strain again through fresh cheesecloth, and bottle. Dip the closed bottles in paraffin to seal, or refrigerate and use quickly.

Mushroom Quiche

(See basic quiche directions, page 180.) Set the oven at 350°F. Into a raw pie shell (see pages 180–81) lay ¼ lb. Swiss cheese. Add a custard made of 3 raw eggs, 1½ cups half and half or whole milk, a little salt, and nutmeg, stirred with about 3 cups wild mushrooms sautéed in sparing amounts of butter and oil, or brushed with butter or oil and roasted. Lay on the top ¼ lb. sharp cheddar, or, if you prefer, a mild cheese, and bake about 1 hour at 350°F, or until the center doesn't jiggle.

Escalloped Mushrooms
(From my grandmother's cookbook, 1898.)

Put the honeycomb mushrooms (undoubtedly she meant morels) in a buttered baking dish with alternate layers of crumbs, seasoning each layer plentifully with butter; add salt, pepper, and a gill of cream. Bake 20 minutes, keeping covered while in the oven.

FRUITS

The value of these wild fruits is not in the mere possession or eating of them, but in the sight and enjoyment of them. The very derivation of the word "fruit" would suggest this. It is from the Latin fructus, *meaning "that which is used or enjoyed."*

—Henry David Thoreau

The saga of Eric the Red, who visited North America five hundred years before Columbus, mentions salmon larger than any that had ever been seen in Norway, and other wonders of the western land. Tales in Norway shortly after 1000 A.D. told of a land to the west so full of growing things that a man could go there and never have to work another day in his life. "Beer as sweet as Munchener springs from the ground and flows away, the cows all love to milk themselves, and hens lay eggs ten times a day," goes one verse to an old Norwegian folk song called "Oleanna." So promising did the newfound land seem that there, "the poorest knave in Norway becomes a king in a year or so."

Wild fruits were a whole category meriting praise. Fruit has been important food for humans as far back as we can trace. In general, fruits provide vitamins, especially vitamin C. Some nutritionists have opined that fruits are the least consumed of any of the major food groups; difficulty of preparation seems to be the reason. Americans habitually eat a vegetable with the evening meal, but where in our diets is fruit consumed? Further, wild fruit may be the one thing that there is more of now than there was when our forebears first came to this continent.

Native Americans knew and used everything edible in the plant kingdom. Many native fruits were used medicinally as well as for food. The first settlers clung for a while to English medicine, then slowly adopted Native American cures. After the American Revolution, native drugs were, for a time, the only drugs available, and after 1800 the Shakers developed a brisk trade growing and selling American herbs when there was a national resistance to buying medicines from England.

In the late nineteenth century, patent medicines became the rage, made mostly of plant distillations in alcohol. Christian ladies who wouldn't touch a drop of the devil's firewater stayed tipsy all day sipping on their herbal remedies, prescribed by doctors who hadn't a clue about what was wrong with most of them. Any cures may have been attributable to the alcohol rather than the plants. Many of the fruits discussed here were important in folk remedies.

Some excellent fruits are omitted here. Wild gooseberries, for example, are subject on this continent to certain molds, and this makes finding good ones a rarity. Peaches grow wonderfully in America tended in orchards, but a peach untended (in the wild) reverts very quickly to small, inedible fruit useful only "to fatten hogs," according to one disgruntled source.

▣ APPLES

Pyrus (Latin for "pear") is the genus apples, crab apples, pears, and (according to some botanists) quinces belong to. Apples, known to be one of the earliest fruits cultivated by humans, are placed in a subgenus, *Malus* (Latin for "apple").

DESCRIPTION, HABITAT, AND SEASON

There are literally thousands of apple varieties, some of which bear fruit in every season. They grow on long-lived small trees with gnarled, hard, short branchlets, with serrated oblong-ovate leaves, and white to pink fragrant blossoms in the spring. All apples have a cartilagelike covering that protects the seeds. Apples are highly variable in flavor, texture, size, sweetness, and color. The only things they have in common are white or whitish flesh that browns on exposure to air, and that elusive, delightful "appley" odor and flavor.

Though wild apples are apt to be wormy or partially eaten by birds, often these old-fashioned apples have more flavor and sweetness than any of the modern cultivars so large and symmetrical that they hardly look real. (Cultivated varieties of any fruit, bred selectively by man, cannot perpetuate themselves sexually through seeds, and thus do not exist in the wild.) If you can locate two or three good wild trees, they will reward your annual wait with more apples than you can possibly use.

HISTORY AND LORE

Apple trees can live a hundred years, and apples have been eaten by humans for eons. Swiss prehistoric lake dwellers ate crab apples and larger apples, and carbonized remains show that they were sometimes cut in half, as if to be dried for future use.

One of America's favorite legends recounts the journey by John Chapman (born in Boston around 1774), better known as Johnny Appleseed, who set out on his charming and peculiar mission to plant all America with apple trees grown directly from seeds. After 1800 it was rare to find any homestead between the East Coast and the Mississippi without several apple trees. It is clear to any forager that folks used to tend apple trees of different varieties, often quite near to one another. This is because different varieties mature at different times, and are good for different things. Our legacy is that we often have a wide variety of apples to choose from within a fairly small area. Those old-fashioned apples were abandoned when newer, more disease-resistant strains were developed, or when farms just fell into ruin.

Apples are deeply American: Regional cookery gives us New England apple cobblers, Pennsylvania German apple pancakes, Virginia apple candy, Appalachian cider, and southern fried pies. Apple pie is the most American dessert there is.

But for every benefit there is a cost. Though some of the new cultivars like Gala and Braeburn are wonderful, and I buy them at the grocery store, personally, I'd rather pare away the wormy parts of those intense, hard, strong Black Twig or Winesap apples left over from another time than eat a perfectly formed, perfectly tame Golden Delicious from the supermarket.

Although apples have no specific medical uses, they are rich in vitamins and fiber, pectin and minerals, and must be listed among the most famous medicines in the world: Everyone grows up knowing that an apple a day keeps the doctor away.

R E C I P E S

To find out if a wild apple is good for cooking, just steam a few chunks or slices of it, and try it for flavor and consistency. For the forager, trial and error is the method. For instance, after years of looking and testing, we now keep an eye on three wild trees: The first, which ripens and drops its streaky reddish fruit near the end of June, is full of hard apples that taste sour when bitten into, but are absolutely without peer as cooking apples, as they stay firm, have a good strong flavor and tartness, and can be sweetened with sugar. This means that in June I make our year's supply of applesauce, apple butter, apple jelly, and fried apples. We have an August tree along a country road near town, with crisp, hard apples that never blush but are full of rural integrity. The tree we gather from in October and even later is full of dark, black-red apples that are wonderful to eat and make cider out of: so crisp they almost cut your mouth, so juicy and tart-sweet they drip down your chin—but they cook up pappy, mushy, and tasteless. We eat the biggest ones, and make cider or apple jelly out of the rest of them.

Fried Apples

Carefully chop cooking apples. I leave the skins on, for flavor and consistency. If discoloration bothers you, sprinkle the cut apples from time to time with lemon juice. Heat a little butter or margarine, just enough to coat the bottom of the skillet. Add the apples, and sprinkle with sugar, ground cinnamon, and allspice. Stir to distribute the sugar, spice, and fat, cover the pan, and cook over slow heat, stirring occasionally, until the apples are tender. Naturally the amount of sugar can vary enormously, and other spices can be used as well. Scandinavian apple dishes are often seasoned with cardamom, and some people like to add a bit of ground cloves, nutmeg, or ginger. I use brown sugar sometimes in place of white.

Apple Cider

Cider is nothing but chopped or ground apples pressed to force out the liquid, which turns brown immediately upon exposure to air.

For cider, you need some kind of press. A real cider press (now available only in specialty or antiques shops) has gears for grinding up the apples. The pieces fall into a straight-sided wooden bucket with slightly separated slats on the sides and bottom. When the bucket is full, a weight is placed atop the apples, and pressure mechanically applied. The cider is expressed through the slats in the bucket into a trough that carries it to the receiving bucket. The mash is thrown out when no more liquid can be forced from it, and the process is repeated.

Today, an electric juicer can be used to make cider. You could even try a ricer. Grind up the apples, cores and all, and press the pulp in some way to expel the juice. It won't be as efficient as using the real item, but you can make great fresh cider, or use the liquid for apple jelly (instructions for which are found in any box of commercial pectin).

Apple Chutney

An elegant condiment for curries or roast meats. Gather about 3 lbs. tart cooking apples, cut into small chunks, in an enamel cooking pot. Add the following: 1 huge onion, cut into small chunks; 2 to 4 cloves garlic, chopped fine; 1 cup raisins; 1 tsp. salt; 2 tsp. ground cinnamon, 1 tsp. ground ginger, 1 tsp. ground cloves, 1 tsp. dry mustard; 1 cup brown sugar and 1 cup white; and 1 cup cider vinegar. Cook this mixture slowly for about 1 hour, or until it is thick, stirring frequently with a wooden spoon.

▓ CRAB APPLES

Crab apples are varieties of apples with what botanists refer to as "inferior fruit" (fruit that is sour, like a crabby person is sour), and often are planted as ornamental trees today, for their lovely shapes and beautiful foliage. They are natives to America, while apples were introduced by the English.

DESCRIPTION, HABITAT, AND SEASON

Crab apples are small, slender trees with showy blossoms of reddish pink or white in the spring. Later in the year they produce oval, sunset-hued fruits with no depression at the stem end, anywhere from one-third inch in diameter to about an inch and a half. None that I know of is palatable raw.

HISTORY AND LORE

In England in the past, the sour juice of crab apples was sold under the name verjuice, and believed to be a great health enhancer. It must have tasted bad enough to feel like medicine.

RECIPES

Use crab apples just as you would use any other sour apples. The fruit of some ornamental crab apples I found planted at the law school near our house was perfect for my experiment. Nobody ever picked them. I'd seen recipes for crab apple jelly everywhere. I brought home a big basketful of the apples. They sat on the dining room table and scented the whole house with apple. I cooked a handful up, tasted some of the flesh cautiously, decided it was fine if I added sugar, cooked some more up, made crab apple sauce, then crab apple jelly, then pickled crab apples using a method I usually use for Watermelon Rind Pickles.

Pickled Crabs
(See recipe for Watermelon Rind Pickles, pages 168–69.)

Just leave out the lime water soak, and substitute whole crab apples for the rind. It was so successful I plan on doing tons of them next year. The pickled crab apples are beautiful, deep red, and make a tasty and pretty garnish for dinner plates.

Apple/Crab Apple Sauce

First scrub clean apples, or crab apples, and pare them into chunks without worms or beakholes. Do not peel them, but if you prefer, you can remove the cores of the apples. Leave crab apples whole or you'll never finish! Then add just the smallest amount of water, say ½ cup for a big pot of apple chunks or crab apples, and steam them quickly, just until they are tender. Watch them, stir them often, and add water if necessary to prevent scorching. Force the cooked apples or crab apples through a potato masher or a ricer, and add sugar to taste. That's basic applesauce. Serve it hot, cold, or at room temperature. Add cinnamon, nutmeg, allspice, or a combination if you like it spicy.

Apple/Crab Apple Butter

Begin with basic applesauce. You need to add approximately half as much sugar as you have sauce. But taste, and add to your liking. Then, the spices. Start with 1 tsp. each ground cinnamon and ground nutmeg; and ½ tsp. each ground cloves and ground ginger; and 1 split vanilla bean (optional). Adding the spices and sugar slowly is a good idea, for you can add more but you can't take any out. You'll probably need a little more of the spices. When you have it tasting wonderful, cook this mixture slowly, in a pan with a lot of surface (wide and shallow is best), stirring it often to keep it from scorching, tasting it until it's just right (you can add spice or sugar at any time), simmering until it is reduced and thickened to suit you. This shouldn't take very long: 20 minutes to about 1 hour. Taste is the determinant here; as apple butter is a condiment, it should be spicy and sweet. The grown-ups I watched cook as a child had a way to test the readiness: On a clean saucer, spoon about 1 Tbsp. of the hot butter. If it retains its integrity as a puddle, it's ready. If it leaks at the edges, it's not. Try for yourself.

When it is done, take out the vanilla bean if you used one, jar the butter in boiled (sterilized) jars, cap it, and if you like, dip the tops in melted paraffin to seal. Don't forget to date and label each jar.

Crab Apple Jelly

This is something you just can't miss. Find a place with ornamental crab apple trees, and watch for the fruit to ripen. Gather 5 lbs. ripe (they'll still be hard) crab apples. Wash, but do not peel or core. Place in large saucepan, stainless steel or enamel. Add 5 cups water, bring to a boil, cover, and boil until the crab apples split and are soft. Make a double cheesecloth bag by sewing two layers to two more layers on a machine, so that you have a square sewn on three sides. Put the bag in a big bowl, the cooked apples and juice in the bag, and hang the bag up higher than the bowl. Let it drip, or when it is cool enough, press and knead the bag to release more liquid. When you have 7 cups juice, stop. Discard the bag and its contents, or put the pulp on your mulch pile. Measure 9 cups sugar into a separate dry bowl. Stir 1 box fruit pectin into the juice, and bring to a boil, stirring continuously. When it is boiling furiously, threatening to climb to the top of the pot, add the sugar all at once. Return to that furious boil, and boil exactly 1 minute, stirring the whole time. Remove from the stove, skim any foam, and pour quickly into sterilized jars. This makes about 10 cups. To me, it's the best jelly of all.

I made 30 cups of absolutely wonderful crab apple jelly last June when the ornamental crabs fruited and ripened at the law school near our house. The caretaker assured me the fruit was just something else she had to rake up, so I collected a huge basket, took her a jar of the jelly, and everybody was happy.

▣ BLACKBERRIES AND RASPBERRIES

Rubus means "red" in Latin, and is kin, of course, to our word *ruby*. The *Rubus* family includes hundreds of species, subspecies, and cultivars of berries,

Blackberries

all of which look like the native
blackberries (Rubus alleghe-
niensis), or blackberries of
the Allegheny Mountains,
and have solid centers, or
like raspberries (R. idaeus),
which have hollow centers.

DESCRIPTION,
HABITAT, AND
SEASON

The Rubus berries all look
more like a bunch of tiny
fruits glued together than a
single fruit, and in fact, each
tiny segment of each berry does contain a single tiny seed. They all have

Raspberries

serrated gray-green leaves, usually three, five, or seven, and nearly all
of them have prickly stems. Often the leaves are lighter underneath
than on top. Out of season, the old canes, or stalks, reddish, gray, or
greenish blue, show where the berries will be in harvest time. Rubus
ripen from early summer through early fall, depending on the species.
In the mountains of Virginia, I grew up with a berry calendar in my
head: June 20, black raspberries, or black-caps; July 3, wineberries;
July 20, blackberries. Dewberries, or ground blackberries, from mid-
June to mid-August. The seasons never vary more than a few days
either way, though of course the crops vary with rain and sunshine.

Rubus berries are a lot like starlings; they have learned to live anywhere. The edges of woods, the back lots of city buildings, farm
pastures, creek- and riverbanks, fields, vacant city lots, the perimeters
of in-town gardens. All can and do support some kind of Rubus berry.
Birds eat the berries, then distribute the seeds widely, and the seeds
take hold and grow with tenacity.

All of the *Rubus* are edible, wherever they grow, whenever you find them ripe. Though they differ in sweetness, tenderness, and juiciness, all share the characteristic berry flavor. Whether they grow trailing along the ground, on upright stalks, or on arching canes, gather them and remember where you found them so you can come back year after year.

HISTORY AND LORE

Rubus berries hold an honorable and consistent place in folk medicine. Roman use dates from before the second century, when Apuleius published an early herbal and flower book, *Florida,* in which can be found the drawing of a blackberry, *Rubus fruticosus.* Blackberry was believed by Herodotus to cure gout. Teas made from *Rubus* leaves or roots are astringent, and have been used by many primitive peoples. John Gerard's 1597 *The Herball* lists both leaf and fruit of *Rubus* species as astringent.

In this country, the salmonberry *(R. parviflorus)* was used by the Indians of the Pacific Northwest as a food, and in the form of a tea made from the canes as a diuretic. Salmonberry is said to taste better cooked than raw. Ojibwa used black raspberry root tea as well as the berries for stomachache. The Rappahannock Indians of Virginia used the roots and berries steeped as tea to allay diarrhea. Some Indian tribes used blackberry root steeped in water as an eyewash; others favored an eyewash made of a tincture of red raspberry leaves.

In early American medicine, blackberry leaves were believed to counter diabetes, and blackberry root extract was the major ingredient in a seventeenth-century Virginia cholera cure. Tea made from most species' leaves has been used for ages to stanch diarrhea, dysentery, uterine hemorrhage, and sometimes even runny noses. It has even been reported that blackberry leaf juice will fasten loose teeth back into the jaw. Perhaps this is because the astringent juice seemed to pull at the flesh of the mouth, or tighten the flesh around the teeth. Moistened leaves of any *Rubus* plants have been used as poultices to draw bad blood from wounds and festering sores.

Cruso's 1771 *Treasury of Easy Medicine* advises soaking blackberry leaves in hot wine and placing them on ulcers morning and evening.

The fruits have been prescribed to cool fevers. As the berries are slightly laxative (like most fruits), they may offer some measure of relief from constipation. Many of the early settlers believed that the *Rubus* species had special efficacy against "summer complaint," a diarrhea brought on, it was believed, by heat, but more probably by spoiled food in an era before refrigeration.

On August 4, 1804, one James Anderson wrote a testimonial that was printed in the *Philadelphia Medical and Surgical Journal*, Volume I, Pt. 1, in 1805:

> *Last summer, when I was near the settlement of the Oneida-Indians (in the state of New York), the dysentery prevailed much, and carried off some of the white inhabitants, who applied to the Indians for a remedy. They directed them to drink a decoction of the roots of Blackberry-bushes which they did, after which not one died. All who used it agreed, that it is a safe, sure, and speedy cure.*

Blackberries are said to cure anemia. According to the Doctrine of Signatures, the color and/or shape of anything in nature dictates its use to man. Thus yellow plants are useful for kidney problems, and walnuts are beneficial for the brain. By this reasoning, the black-red blackberry juice might darken pale, or anemic, blood. A nineteenth-century commercial gargle for sore throats, "Blackberry Glycerite," combined glycerin and blackberry vinegar. One contemporary midwestern writer described watching her mother dry fresh blackberries in a low oven, and grind them to a powder, to be used as a diarrhea remedy, in this century. The powder was to be taken, she wrote, a teaspoon at a time, stirred into hot water. A medicine named "Blackberry Balsam" was marketed in this country as a diarrhea remedy, from 1846 until well into the twentieth century. In this century, blackberry juice been used to stamp the appropriate grades on inspected U.S. Department of Agriculture meats.

It was the June I graduated from Hollins, 1959. That summer I invested a large percentage of my salary for my first paid teaching job on my first car, a wrecked-but-still-mobile 1940 Plymouth.

Nothing on the car ever worked very well. My memory of that summer is of many suitors, interested chiefly in Gerontion, for that was what I named the car, from T. S. Eliot's poem about an old man. Each beau yearned to solve its mysteries, to be the one who would finally make it work. While Harry, Sam, Scotty, Ralph, or Rick performed surgery under the hood, I brush-painted it a wonderful metallic 1959 turquoise blue color, and it shone burnished and streaky. I hammered out its dented fender, which gave its contours the pocked appearance of a turquoise orange. When I had finished, I made flowered seat covers for it, to cover the holes from the first owner's dropped cigarettes.

But one day in midsummer Gerontion stopped, sighed, and sat down on the job somewhere on a country road. My friend Jeanne and I had been swimming at Goshen Pass; we had no clothes but the bathing suits and tennis shoes we were wearing. We started walking toward town to find a telephone, calmly because by then such behavior on the car's part had become Standard Operating Procedure, and who knew what wild game we might be able to flush out to come rescue us?

Suddenly around a curve there appeared a lush patch of ripe black raspberries just beyond the fence at the edge of the road. We looked around, and in the roadside honeysuckle we found an old chrome hubcap. So in we plunged, holding the barbed wires apart for each other, determined to pick as many berries as we could eat there and carry home in our hubcap and our four hands. Gingerly we made our way through the patch, the laden wickets springing together like a magic forest behind us. We were well away from the road and surrounded by the dense bushes when a bellow caused us to look up. Coming at us, fast, in hide considerably thicker than ours, was one mad cow, with horns.

We arrived safely back on the road, mostly just shaken and scratched up, and stained. We walked on to find a farmhouse, called up some boys who gladly came out to fetch us and make the car run again, and deliver us to the doctor's office.

As we were getting tetanus shots some hours later and having our brier-and-barbed-wire wounds scoured clean by a grumpy nurse, we tried to figure out what had been wrong with that cow. It was not a bull. We were country girls, and knew the difference. Bovine hormones? A calf hidden nearby? All we could ever conclude was that it must have been her berry patch. She liked black raspberries as well as we did, and we hadn't asked permission.

The dried bark of the rhizome and roots of *Rubus* plants was on the official United States Pharmaceutical List from 1820 until 1916, as an astringent and tonic. Today the berries are still a popular flavoring for medicines. *Rubus* leaves have been analyzed and found to contain useful amounts of tannin, an astringent.

Some Indian tribes found the soft leaves of some *Rubus* species useful as toilet paper.

Most recently, a substance in the leaves of red raspberries called framamine, or fragrine, or fragerine, isolated in the 1940s, strengthens, relaxes, and tones the uterus, thus exonerating the old wives' advice that raspberry leaf tea be taken throughout pregnancy, labor, and postparturition. The leaves, according to modern analysis, are high in magnesium, which is still in use to prevent miscarriage.

Another tea, which is antiscorbutic, a tonic for the uterus, and febrifuge, is made by crushing the dried root (gathered in the fall). One tablespoon of the crushed dried root is added to a pint of boiling water. When it is cool, it is ready to use, though folk sources are not in agreement on how much and how often.

R E C I P E S

Blackberry Jelly

Gather ripe, underripe, and green blackberries, cover with a little water, and simmer until soft. Squeeze or drip through a jelly bag to make 4 cups juice. Measure 4 cups sugar, and stir it into the juice until dissolved. Bring to a full boil, add a pea-size lump of butter, and boil until jelled, which will only take a bit of time. This is really superior to any other berry jelly I have ever tasted. But you do need about a quarter of your berries to be green or underripe.

Berry Mousse

Sprinkle 1 envelope gelatin in $\frac{1}{4}$ cup water, and set aside. Boil 1 cup water and 1 cup sugar together for 5 minutes. Add the gelatin and stir until dissolved. Add 1 quart or more berries, picked over and washed, and cook just until soft, under 5 minutes. Strain the berries and syrup through a sturdy sieve, ricer, or cheesecloth, to remove seeds. Add the juice of 1 lemon, stir thoroughly, and set aside. When the mix is warm-cool, beat 4 egg whites until stiff, and fold into the berries. Then beat until stiff and fold in 1 cup whipping cream with 1 tsp. vanilla and 1 Tbsp. sugar. Pour into a fancy dish, and refrigerate several hours, until it's jelled. A variation on this is to use flavored gelatin, 1 small box, low calorie or regular. Lemon is always a good choice, but you could use strawberries with strawberry gel, or raspberries with raspberry gel, or raspberries with lemon gel, or blackberries with raspberry gel—your choice. And great news for calorie watchers: The sugar-free gelatin desserts taste just as good in this mousse as the sugared.

Iced Raspberry Vinegar

This was a popular summer drink at the end of the last century. It's worth a try, and you may even like it. Mix water, sugar or honey, and raspberry (or blackberry) vinegar to taste (see the recipe under "Strawberries," page 113), and serve over ice for a refreshing summer ade. It's a sort of forerunner of Gatorade.

▦ BLUEBERRIES AND HUCKLEBERRIES

Blueberries, many different species, belong to the *Vaccinium* genus. The genus name, kin to our word *vaccination,* comes from a Latin word for "cows," and probably designates the location of many of the berries: pastures.

Blueberries

The huckleberry, dangleberry, sunberry, or wonderberry is technically one of several varieties of the *Gaylussacia* genus, named for its discoverer, a nineteenth-century French chemist named Gay-Lussac.

DESCRIPTION, HABITAT, AND SEASON

Huckleberry plants grow two to five feet high, and frequent swamps, woodlands, roadsides, and especially burned-over

Huckleberries

ground. The *Gaylussacia* are close kin to the *Vaccinium*, and to the untutored eye look the same. However, having said that, it is a fact that blueberries and huckleberries are generally indistinguishable to the foraging eye as well.

Many plant books show one of several *Vaccinium*, and call it huckleberry; in fact the word *huckleberry* is a corruption of whortleberry, a name for the blueberry. Confused? Don't worry. They're all good to eat. Botanically, the difference lies in how many teensy seeds are in each berry (ten in *Gaylussacia*, four or five in *Vaccinium*). But as the seeds are virtually too small to count, it really isn't necessary to distinguish between the berries.

The way we get from *cow* to *vaccination* is that during the time people were dying of smallpox, dairymaids, who worked around cows, often got a milder pox called cowpox. In 1796, Edward Jenner, an observant physician, noticed that they *never* got smallpox afterward. He reasoned that if everyone could get a case of cowpox, they'd wipe out smallpox. He invented vaccinations, made of cowpox serum, and eventually the world was freed of the great disfiguring and devastating scourge of smallpox.

Blueberries are larger, lighter in color, and "dustier" than huckle-berries, which are by contrast smaller, darker, shinier, and purpler than blueberries.

Blueberries and huckleberries, which grow throughout temperate North America, and ripen in mid- to late summer, are small (one-quarter to one-half inch), blue to deep purple to black, on insignificant little shrubs with small, oval, dark green leaves. Euell Gibbons claims to have picked swamp huckleberries in New Jersey on bushes fifteen feet high, and my friend from New Hampshire says her blueberry bushes stand about five feet tall. In Virginia, where they are sometimes called buckberries, I've never seen a blueberry or huckleberry bush higher than three feet, and they're usually closer to eighteen inches.

The highbush blueberry, *Vaccinium corymbosum,* is the most common blueberry of our New England states, the berry dark blue with a bloom (a dusty or powdery look).

Huckleberries grow spars-ely, on spare bushes twelve to eighteen inches high, in sandy soil, scraggly woods, ripening on or about the first of August. In general, the places to look for blueber-ries and huckleberries are open fields, any area that has recently been burned over, along country roads, and on sandy paths at the edge of sparse woods, for they will only grow in wide-open scrubby areas, and they like light soil and sunshine all day long.

Go out with a bucket in late summer and pick whatever looks like a blueberry or huckleberry. If you find a laden bush, lay a sheet under it and shake it for a clean, fast harvest.

> . . . At this hour a goodly number
> of blueberries decide to ripen.
> Once they were wax white.
> Then came the green of small bruises.
> After that, the red of bad welts.
> All this time they enlarged themselves.
> Now they are true blue. . . .
>
> —Maxine Kumin, a New Hampshire Pulitzer Prize–winning poet, describes the ripening of blueberries, in "The Hermit Picks Berries"

HISTORY AND LORE

Although they are similar and interchangeable, there are semantic differences between blueberries and huckleberries. Blueberries are usually associated with New England and the Midwest, while huckleberries are considered southern. Blueberries provided the dye for the navy blue garments of New England whalers. Huckleberry Finn, one of America's most-loved literary characters, is wild and southern. Remember, too, how Robert McClosky's Sal gathered blueberries in Maine, while Br'er Rabbit, from the southern brier patch, stole Br'er Fox's huckleberry jam.

RECIPES

Blueberry Buckle

Preheat oven to 375°F. Assemble 1 stick butter, $1\frac{1}{4}$ cups sugar, 1 egg, $2\frac{1}{3}$ cups self-rising flour (or $2\frac{1}{3}$ cups flour with 2 tsp. baking powder and $\frac{1}{2}$ tsp. salt stirred in thoroughly), $\frac{1}{2}$ cup milk, 2 cups blueberries, and $\frac{1}{2}$ tsp. cinnamon. Cream half the stick of butter with $\frac{3}{4}$ cup of the sugar. Beat in the egg. Add 2 cups of the self-rising flour (or flour mix) alternately with $\frac{1}{2}$ cup milk. Fold in the washed blueberries. Pour the batter into a greased 9" × 9" pan. Sprinkle the top with crumb topping made by fork-blending the remaining 4 Tbsp. butter, $\frac{1}{2}$ cup sugar, $\frac{1}{3}$ cup flour, and $\frac{1}{2}$ tsp. cinnamon. Bake 35 minutes at 375°F. You will see how the top "buckles" and understand its name.

Blueberry Coffee Cake

Preheat oven to 350°F. Assemble 2 cups biscuit mix, $\frac{1}{2}$ cup sugar, $\frac{1}{3}$ cup safflower oil or melted butter or margarine, 2 eggs, 1 cup milk. Mix the dry ingredients thoroughly. Mix the liquids well. Mix the two lightly, and pour into a square 9" pan. Over this place the topping, which is 2 cups blueberries, $\frac{1}{2}$ cup sugar, $\frac{1}{2}$ tsp. cinnamon, $\frac{1}{2}$ tsp. allspice, and 4 Tbsp. melted butter, tossed together. Bake until done, about 45 minutes.

Huckleberry Cake with Hard Sauce
(The favorite summer recipe of my childhood.)

Turn on the oven to 375°F. Cream ¾ stick butter, 1 tsp. vanilla, and 1 cup sugar. Add 2 big eggs, well beaten, and beat mixture well. Mix and sift 1¾ cups flour, ½ tsp. salt, and 2 tsp. baking powder. Measure ½ cup milk. Alternately add flour and milk to the creamed ingredients, beating until the batter is smooth and thoroughly mixed. Flour 2 cups berries by tossing them in 2 or 3 Tbsp. flour until all are coated. Pour into a sieve and shake gently to remove extra flour. Fold into the yellow cake batter. Bake in a buttered loaf pan at 375°F for about 45 minutes, while dinner is being eaten. Serve the cake hot, in slices, with a generous dollop of cold Hard Sauce (recipe follows). A yellow cake mix works fine, too. Add the floured berries at the end of the mixing time.

Hard Sauce

With an electric beater, cream ¾ stick room-temperature butter, and slowly add 2 Tbsp. cream, 1 Tbsp. each brandy, rum, and sherry, and ½ tsp. vanilla until smooth. Little by little add 1 lb. of confectioners' sugar, more or less, until the mixture is rich and smooth and homogenized. It should hold a shape. You can do this quickly in a blender or food processor. Mound it in a dish, grate half a fresh nutmeg over the top, and chill until serving time. Top each hot slice of cake generously with hard sauce.

Peach-Blueberry Cobbler

Turn the oven to 350°F. Mix together 8 peaches, peeled, pitted, and sliced, with 1 pint blueberries or huckleberries, 2 Tbsp. lemon juice, 3 Tbsp. cornstarch, and 1 cup sugar. Pour into a shallow casserole to make a bottom layer. Make the crumbly topping and crumble it over the fruit: 6 Tbsp. margarine, 1 cup sugar, 2 tsp. vanilla, ½ cup flour, 1 cup old-fashioned rolled oats, and 1 tsp. ground cinnamon. Bake the dessert until the top is nicely browned, about 1 hour. Serve it hot with vanilla ice cream or frozen yogurt on top.

▨ CHERRIES

Pin cherry, wild cherry, bird cherry, choke cherry, fireberry, and chokeberry are some of the folk names of various small berrylike drupes of the *Prunus* genus, which is that genus of fruits with a single stone. *Prunus* is kin to our word *prune,* which is of course a dried plum.

DESCRIPTION, HABITAT, AND SEASON

Cherry trees are small trees or shrubs; they have erect or trailing branches, opposite long, thin, shiny, single, serrated leaves, and lovely five-petaled white or pink blossoms in the spring. They are a Temperate Zone fruit, and ripen in late summer. All cherries, red, black, purple, or yellow, have a round, globular, single seed in the middle, and grow on stems. They vary in size from blueberrry or pea size to an inch in diameter.

There are many wild cherries, and they all yield fruit, some better than others, some sweet and some bitter. The ripe fruit of all cherry trees is safe. Let taste be your guide.

HISTORY AND LORE

Grocery store cherries are cultivars from *P. cerasus* (Latin for "cherry"), brought to America from Europe, brought to Europe from Asia in ancient times. (This is why you don't find cherry trees in the wild with fruits that look like cherries you'd find in the grocery store.)

Lucullus, remembered today for the splendor of his banquets, is believed to have introduced cherries to Italy. Perhaps this is why cherries have always been an elite fruit to man.

Cherries are all technically poisonous, for the leaves, pits, bark, and twigs are all loaded with cyanide. But the flesh of the drupe, which has no poison, is one of man's favorite fruits, and cherry is an extremely popular aroma in candies, wines, liqueurs, preserves, cough drops, and pies, as well as in perfumes and room deodorants. The roots were sought by Indians, scraped and boiled, to make a soothing wash for abrasions, and a tea for stomach troubles. Wild cherry bark is an ingredient in many cough syrups even today. Indeed, my own grandmother made such a remedy, with a teaspoon of the inner bark shaved into a cup of boiling water, adding honey as a sweetener. But this is not recommended, as the amateur forager has no way of knowing how much bark is too much.

Some folks are fond of the almond flavor in fruit seeds that warns of the presence of cyanide. In my childhood, many housewives added a peach pit seed, which looks just like an almond, as flavoring to each jar of peach preserves they made, and a few cherry seeds to each jar of cherry preserves. A family I knew ate several seeds from each apple they ate, believing that the seeds were somehow protective against disease. In fact, laetrile, made of the seed of a cherry-almond-peach-apricot relative, contains cyanide and yet many believe it is effective as a cancer cure.

Wild cherry wine is used in Appalachia as a diarrhea cure as well as a popular homemade beverage. The Italian liqueur Amaretto has crushed cherry seeds as an ingredient.

Because wild cherries are more seed than flesh, they are mostly fun to just eat out of hand while spitting out the seeds. (Swallowing a single cherry seed will not harm anyone, or we would all be dead; it's large amounts that do damage. Besides, the cyanide-containing seed is enclosed in its hard shell covering.) But if you manage to bring home a lot of cherries, you can make a delicious wild cherry sauce for pancakes or ice cream. If you want to enhance the flavor of peaches or cherries, I suggest using a little almond extract from the supermarket.

R E C I P E S

Cherry Sauce

Cook whole, washed cherries until tender in a little water. Once they are soft, to remove the pits, put them in a ricer or potato masher and mash them. The flesh will be pressed through the ricer, coming out sort of like cranberry sauce, leaving the pits and skins in the ricer. Heat this sauce with sugar to taste, and you have cherry sauce. You can make a jam out of this cherry flesh by adding an equal amount of sugar and the juice of 1 lemon, and slowly cooking it to an agreeable thickness, stirring often to prevent scorching.

Cherry Bounce

The grandfather of one of my friends made this, and we stole it as kids and drank it and got giggly.

Stem and pick over 1 gallon wild cherries, any type. Mash them in a crock with some of the shattered seeds included (about 12 to 20). Add 3 lbs. sugar, 1 gallon good whiskey, and 1 pint brandy. Cover tightly and let stand for 2 weeks or so in a dark closet. Strain and bottle. As I recall, this was outstanding.

CRANBERRIES

Vaccinium vitis-idaea or *V. macrocarpon*, bog cranberries, are familiar to Americans. The wild fruits taste identical to the cultivated variety we eat at Thanksgiving, which is to say, sour. They are part of the same genus as blueberries, and their names describe them: *Vaccinium vitis-idaea* suggests that the fruit is of the cow pasture, and looks like grapes *(vitis)* of Mount Ida, which is on Crete. The name of the second variety tells us that they have "great fruit," or *macro carpon*. They are still not as big as the commercial cranberries we can buy, but are well worth the effort to gather them.

DESCRIPTION, HABITAT, AND SEASON

Cranberry plants are evergreen, and have tiny leaves. They have skinny branches, with the fruit-bearing branches erect but still low (half a foot to a foot). In *V. macrocarpon*, the spring-to-summer flowers are white to pinkish, and bell shaped, and the plant usually occurs with water within reach of the root. Cranberries prefer a cool to cold climate, sandy soil, and protected locations, and grow most abundantly from Cape Cod south to New Jersey, and across to Wisconsin. The most likely place to find them is on the borders of ponds, down low where they can find protection from freezing, with the red berries ripening from fall through winter by the water's edge. In *V. vitis-idaea*, the red berries grow on a low, creeping evergreen trailing shrub, generally no more than three inches high, and both the leaves and the berries tend to be small, the fruit somewhat smaller than the cranberries found in markets, which have been pampered and protected and fed vitamins.

HISTORY AND LORE

The Indians gave the scurvy-wracked English the tart red berries to eat after their long ocean voyage to New England. The Indians' *ibimi*, as they called the berries, literally saved the English adventurers' lives, and must have seemed like a miracle food. We know now that cranberries, fruiting after most fresh foods are past harvest, are rich in ascorbic acid, vitamin C, the only vitamin humans cannot store, and thus need daily for bountiful health. The effects of scurvy are reversed quickly with the addition of vitamin C to the diet.

The Indians drank cranberry juice and cranberry tea, and made cranberry bread. They showed white men how to make cranberry sauce or jam (sweetened with maple sugar) to accompany venison. The East Coast Algonquians made an early fast food out of cranberries, called pemmican, as

When Ponce de León and his sailors, long at sea without fresh produce and suffering the aches and stiffness, the loose teeth and enervation, of scurvy, disembarked in Florida, the first thing they did was to gorge themselves on fresh fruits and green plants. The second thing they did was to jump in some of those glorious springs that dot Florida, to get clean after months at sea. The antiscorbutic effects went to work at once, and they began to feel much better quickly. They'd had fruit before, but they'd never seen springs like those. They attributed their restored youths to the clear, crystal waters, and believed they had found the Fountain of Youth.

traveling fare for their seasonal migrations. Pemmican was made of ground cornmeal, dried salted venison, bear fat or some other suet, and dried cranberries, blueberries, or even serviceberries, all made into little patties and cooked on fire-heated rocks. These brilliant little powerhouses of nutrition contained meat, fat, grain, and fruit, a small amount of sugar from the berries, plus the concentrated vitamin C of the dried sour berries. Pemmican could withstand rough treatment, travel efficiently, and last without spoilage.

The Indians' use of cranberries included poulticing wounds with the roasted berries. Cranberries were believed to be effective against poison arrow wounds, and perhaps they were, as the berries are astringent, especially when raw. Cranberries have been praised for easing cramps and childbirth, even convulsions, "hysteria," and "fits." Other early American writers noted that cranberry tea overcomes nausea.

The New England settlers, recognizing a good commercial venture when they saw one, set about to systematically search out and gather the pretty red fruit, wasting no time in providing ships' crews with dried cranberries for voyages across the Atlantic for the next two centuries. Wild cranberries soon became a major money crop in New England, and of course continued to provide one way of getting through the New England winters in good health. Soon cultivated varieties provided bigger and better berries.

Today cranberries symbolize Thanksgiving as surely as turkey does, and have graced our harvest tables ever since the Indians introduced the English to this fruit.

R E C I P E S

My Maine nieces tell me they know how to tell a ripe cranberry from either an unripe one or an overripe one. They bounce them: The green ones bound away at once, and the soft, or overripe, ones more or less just lie there. The good cranberries bounce lightly right into their hands. Thus they collect only the good cranberries for their sauce or juice.

Cranberry Sauce

We still make it about the same way today as the Indians did. Cranberries pop as they cook, which signals that they are done.

Bring to a boil together 4 cups cranberries, 2 cups sugar, 1 cup water. Boil for 10 minutes, or until the bursting of the berries stops, stirring occasionally. Pour at once into a mold and refrigerate until it is jelled. The large amount of pectin in the berries causes the jelly to set.

Orange-Cranberry Conserve

Assemble 1 large orange, 4 cups uncooked cranberries, 2 cups sugar. Cut the orange into chunks, removing all the seeds carefully, but leaving half the skin on. Grind the orange or quickly chop it in a food processor. Quickly chop the cranberries. Stir both together, and add the sugar, stirring thoroughly. Refrigerate for at least 1 day, preferably 2, to let the sugar dissolve before serving.

▣ ELDERBERRIES

The elderberry, *Sambucus canadensis, S. nigrum, S. racemosa,* is a delicious drupe, black when ripe, and the size of a small pea. The name is a Latin word derived from the Greek word for a harp or other musical instrument. The American Indians, half a world away, called elderberries music trees, because the stems made wonderful flutes.

DESCRIPTION, HABITAT, AND SEASON

Elderberry species are shrubs that grow in wet woods and near creeks and rivers throughout all fifty of the United States, and are members of the honeysuckle family. The annual branches die down to the ground each winter. This characteristic helps identify the plant. Elderberry is a stoloniferous plant, which means the roots send out new shoots near the original plant, making thick stands of the plant. Thus elderberry grows in dense thickets of five- to ten-foot-high bushes of many branches. The leaves are compound, opposite, with five to eleven leaflets, pointed and serrated. Elderberry stems are so pulpy they were hollowed out not only for flutes and whistles but also as blowguns and syringes in past times. The bark as well grows in easily detachable tubes.

In spring the off-white, sweet-smelling flowers are born in a flat bunch rather like Queen Anne's lace. The shrubs yield small, flat clusters of blue-black, three-seeded drupes in late summer. *Avoid the red-fruited elderberry* (S. pubens) *with the berries in dome-shaped clusters; that one is poisonous.*

HISTORY AND LORE

Folklore credits the elderberry plant with magical properties, among them the ability to confer invisibility and second sight, and to cure the bites of mad dogs. Elder is said in Celtic mythology to be the tree of compassion. Elderberries were believed by Culpeper and Gerard to restore youth; perhaps this is because gray hair can be restored to black by a dye made from the dwarf elder bush.

RECIPES

Though the stems, roots, and leaves of elderberries are poisonous, the spring flowers and the ripe fruit are delicious and safe. Elderberries and their flowers are still made into wine today by country folks here and in Europe; an Italian liqueur, Sambuca, is flavored with the ripe berries; elderberry pie and elderberry wine are common in Appalachia.

While ripe elderberries are an excellent fruit when cooked— personally, I think they have the best flavor for pie of any berry— eating unripe or uncooked elderberries can cause vomiting and diarrhea. Ripe elderberries are high in vitamins A and C, potassium, iron, and plant protein.

The spring flower heads are popularly dipped into pancake batter and deep-fried into fritters—hence the folk name fritter tree. The flowers can be dried for a mild, pleasant herbal tea; and in the early fall, when you find the berries turned from green to red to black, they make a wonderfully flavorful pie, with a rich, spicy, grapy flavor.

Elder-Flower Fritters

Mix a thin pancake batter. Heat 1 quart vegetable oil to 380°F, dip a branch of the flower heads into the batter, drip or shake off excess batter, and fry quickly. Repeat. I use 1 packet biscuit or pancake mix stirred with 1 cup milk.

Elderberry Pie

Preheat oven to 350°F. Make a double piecrust according to the directions on pages 180–81. Mix 1 quart ripe picked elderberries thoroughly with 1 heaping cup sugar, 1 Tbsp. cornstarch, 1 Tbsp. lemon juice or cider vinegar, and 3 Tbsp. melted butter. Pour them in the bottom crust. Cover with the top crust. Press the top and bottom crusts together, make some slits in the top to let steam escape, and bake the pie until golden.

▨ FIGS

Figs *(Ficus carica)* have escaped into the wild, and spread south-ward from the mid-Atlantic states to the extreme southern parts of this country, but because a single dip to thirty-two degrees will kill a fig, the trees are rare farther north than the Carolinas. *Ficus* means "fig" in Latin; Caria in Asia Minor was its habitat in ancient times. The Carian method of preserving figs for export gives us the dried figs we buy in markets today. Fresh figs are hardly ever found in markets because they are extremely delicate, and no way has yet been found to ship them fresh safely.

Description, Habitat, and Season

Ficus carica is a large spreading shrub or a small tree, with three to five lobed, large leaves; a sweet, soft, fleshy fruit striped on the outside and pink on the inside; and soft, edible seeds throughout the flesh. Fig trees do flower, but the blossom, from which the fruit develops, is so insignificant as to go unnoticed. If frost kills a fig tree, stolons (root sprouts) arise from the ground to begin anew their climb toward the sun. Thus figs in the wild may be found in tight, sprawling patches. (This low growth also helps protect them from frost.) Figs ripen in late summer. An ancient practice still used by fig growers as a ripening aid is to touch the end or "eye" of the fig with oil.

My father, whose favorite fruit was figs, decided he would grow them in Virginia, although he knew that was virtually impossible. He used to treat his single fig tree better than he treated the rest of us: He built a stone terrace for it, and planted it in a protected southwest-facing ell of our Shenandoah Valley house (which I suspect he planned with that fig tree in mind). On winter nights, he'd haul out mountains of old quilts, parkas, and tarps, and wrap blankets over and around its low, spreading limbs. He'd make charcoal fires and set them in buckets near it, and go out in the night to worry over the shrub. If you looked out an upper window, you could see his breath in great puffs in the air, and his bare feet sticking out from under his overcoat as he patted and pushed and tucked that tree around. Most years he succeeded in getting a pretty good crop of figs, which he kept count of and did not share except most grudgingly. But one hard frost would ruin the crop for the next season.

History and Lore

This plant of warm locations appears often in ancient manuscripts, and is most common in Asia, and eastern and southern Europe. The Bible mentions figs often, and we know the Greeks and the Romans cultivated these sweet, pulpy fruits, as their descendants today still do. Figs were once so common that they became objects of contempt: *I don't give a fig,* people say, even today. The Romans ate and used them extensively, and Pliny, who is our authority on what the Romans ate, mentioned thirty varieties.

Today, figs are more often than not relegated to the category of a laxative, and so they were employed from ancient times, but to label them thus does figs a disservice, for they truly are a delicious fruit, one that many people never have the chance to taste fresh. The only way most people eat figs is in the popular confection called Fig Newtons.

R E C I P E S

When I was a child living in San Diego, we had a fig tree out back of our house, and the figs, pink and seedy and sweet as honey inside, were the best fruit I ever ate. They can be grown in hothouses, and even in the mountains of Virginia, but it's difficult.

Fig Ice Cream
(Daddy's idea of heaven.)

Combine 1 quart figs, chopped, 1 cup honey, 1 quart heavy cream, 1 Tbsp. vanilla. Mix and freeze. Three times during the freezing, take out as the sides begin to chill, pour back into the bowl, and beat with a wooden spoon until smooth.

Figgy Pudding

This is a favorite dessert for holidays in Great Britain, made the old-fashioned way. This is from an 1888 cookbook. I used dried figs (Carian figs), as I suspect they have always had to do in England. It's a dessert you ought to try once.

Assemble ½ cup brown sugar, ½ cup finely chopped beef suet, 1 cup chopped apple, 1 cup chopped figs, ½ cup milk, ½ cup dry bread crumbs, 2 separated eggs, ¾ cup flour, and brandy. Add the sugar to the suet, apple, and figs. Pour the milk over the bread crumbs, and add the yolks, well beaten. Combine mixtures, add the flour, then the whites beaten stiff. Turn into a greased pudding mold, and steam in a covered steamer for 4 hours. (I did this by placing the pudding casserole into my pasta pot, adding water halfway up the casserole, and covering with the lid. I continued to add boiling water during the cooking time, to keep it about level.) Finally, this steamed pudding is soaked with as much brandy as it will hold, for several hours before serving, then set on fire to be brought to the table. You can substitute margarine or butter for the suet, though that will change the taste.

▦ GRAPES

Grapes are one of earth's most ubiquitous plants. The genus name, *Vitis,* is from the Latin word for "life," and kin to our words *vital* and *vitality.* All grapes, whether gold, pale green, purple, brown, or red, grow in clusters on vines, and have the characteristic leaves. Some are seedless, but most have seeds in the center of each fruit. The grapes themselves range in size, depending on the variety, from less than half an inch in diameter to over an inch in diameter. They range from tasteless to extremely sweet, fragrant, and tasty. Grapes grow worldwide, there are more than one hundred varieties, and there are thousands of subvarieties. On our side of the Atlantic, wild grapes including *Vitis labrusca,* which means "wild vine," *V. riparia,*

> Always eat grapes downward—that is, always eat the best grapes first; in this way there will be none better left on the bunch, and each grape will seem good down to the last. If you eat the other way, you will not have a good grape in the lot.
>
> —Samuel Butler

or "riverbank vine," *V. vulpina,* the fox grape, and *V. aestivalis,* the summer grape, flourished all along the Atlantic Coast when the white man sighted land in the 1600s.

If a wild grape tastes all right, it is all right. There is one poisonous look-alike: the bitter, unpalatable Canada moonvine, with bitter berries that at first glance might look like a grapevine, but it has no tendrils. Further, if you taste one of the acrid, bitter berries, you will not be tempted to eat them. Finally, moonvine berries contain one sickle-shaped seed; grape seeds are always tear shaped.

DESCRIPTION, HABITAT, AND SEASON

So familiar are the leaves, the coiling tendrils, the sinuous forked vines, and the grapes themselves that any description seems excessive. The heart-shaped leaves are four to six inches in diameter, not serrated, but are often deeply indented to form three lobes.

The best grapes are those that get full sun, so the vines may climb high in trees, thus putting the grapes tantalizingly out of reach. Grapes ripen in late summer or early autumn. Grapevines can be identified in winter by their irregular ropy stems, and the little coiled tendrils that cling even when the plant is dormant.

HISTORY AND LORE

In 986 Viking sailors returning to Scandinavia reported that there lay a land far to the west, beyond the land they called Greenland, whose splendors were such that, a hundred miles at sea, the scent of the ripening grapes could be detected by the

In the *Aeneid,* the hero Aeneas received a typical puzzling oracular message that said, in effect, that he and his wandering sailors would know their new native land by this sign: that they would consume their plates along with their food. One night on the shores of Latium (Italy), Aeneas glanced up and saw that his men were eating the vine leaves that they had used to hold the roasted meat from the fire, by which he realized that they had arrived at their new home.

weary sailors. This story gave rise to the name they gave to the western continent: Vinland, or vine-land.

Grapes are generally believed to be among the earliest of all cultivated fruits. Their country of origin is unknown, but suspected to be the fertile crescent between the Tigris and Euphrates. Grapes have been blessed and cursed throughout history, for their devilish ability to addle human reason while at the same time providing so much pleasure. Grapes average a life span nearly the same as the people who enjoy them, and there is one vine seven hundred years old at Hampton Court Palace outside of London, claimed to be the oldest grapevine in the world.

Grapes are mentioned more frequently in the Bible than any other fruit. Among the ancient Romans, Bacchus, the god of wine, was reputed to have discovered it by accident, and was rewarded by the Etruscans with god status. Cato the Censor wrote that the custom of kissing as greeting between kinfolk began with men attempting to discover if their wives had been drinking in their absence.

Grapes were believed in both ancient Europe and pre-English America to be "eye clearing." Hildegard von Bingen in the twelfth century said that anyone with blurry eyes should lubricate the eyelids daily with the drops that come from the vine after cutting. Grapes were believed to be antiscorbutic and refrigerant (cooling to fevers). Dark grapes like the Concord provided, and still do, a purple dye for wool.

Thomas Jefferson, a moderate drinker, was concerned with the widespread drunkenness of Virginians during his time, and the easy availability of hard liquors. It was always Jefferson's belief that a healthy wine industry would prove an antidote to the drunkenness that plagued colonial life from the beginning. Water being the most dangerous beverage of all in Europe, the immigrants were cautious about drinking water in the New World, too. From the beginning, brandies were made from wild fruits, liquor from corn, and being in a constant state of inebriation helped buffer the miserable colonists against the rigors of frontier life: cold, boredom, too much salted meat, and too little in the way of medical services.

R E C I P E S

In the cuisine of eastern Europe and throughout the Middle East are certain dishes that use the large, tender leaves of grapevines (picked in the spring) to enclose meat or rice mixtures. The Indians of North America ate wild grapes, and also used them for medicine. Seminole Indians stuffed fish with grapes before cooking them; the Iroquois stuffed ducks and other game birds with grapes and roasted them.

Recent research gives us the go-ahead on moderate wine drinking, especially red wine (which is red because the grape skins are used in its making). A substance in wine called resveratrol helps to reduce cholesterol and lower blood pressure. Of interest here is that wild grapes and wine grapes have more resveratrol than supermarket eating grapes; the speculation is that the table grapes are so coddled in their raising that they fail to produce the substance, which guards the wild grapes and wine grapes from disease.

Grape Juice

Remove wild grapes from their stems, throwing out any grapes that are rotten. For 5 lbs. grapes, add about 1 cup water. Heat slowly to a boil but do not crush the grapes. Make a cheesecloth lining (two layers) in a colander or sieve, and pour the boiled grapes into the sieve. Let the grapes drip for 1 hour. You can gently move the cheesecloth to facilitate the dripping, but don't squeeze or the juice will be cloudy. Add sugar to sweeten and drink fresh or refrigerate for up to 1 week, or use the grape juice for jelly.

Dolmades
(Stuffed Grape Leaves)

In the spring, when the leaves are full grown but still tender, choose 24 large, perfect grape leaves. Wash them thoroughly, and lay them one on top of the other, in a pan. Add 1 cup water, 1 cup vinegar, 1 cup salt. Bring them to a boil, and boil gently for 5 minutes. Remove from heat and leave overnight in the brine. Next day, they are ready to use.

Stuffing for Dolmades
(This is typically Greek, but you can modify it.)

Assemble 1 cup cooked rice; 1 Tbsp. olive oil; 1 lb. ground beef or lamb; 1 onion, finely chopped; 1 clove garlic, finely chopped; ½ tsp. dried dill weed; salt; pepper; 1 Tbsp. catsup or tomato paste; ⅛ tsp. each cinnamon, nutmeg, allspice; ¼ cup chopped parsley. Reserve the rice. Heat the olive oil, and add the meat, onion, garlic, and spices to it. Cook, stirring, until the meat has lost any red color. Add the cooked rice, mix well, and there is your stuffing. In the center of each grape leaf, place 2 Tbsp. of the mixture. Fold the sides in first, then roll the grape leaf into a neat, fat envelope, entirely covering the stuffing. Place them seam side down tightly nestled side by side in a pan, add 1 cup water, cover tightly, and bake 1 hour at about 350°F. When taking them out of the pan, handle them carefully so as not to unwrap or pierce the envelopes.

Spiced Wild Grape Jelly for Venison

Assemble 1 quart ripe wild grapes, plus about 1 cup unripe grapes, 1 cup cider vinegar, 1 Tbsp. whole cloves, 1 stick cinnamon, broken, and 1 lb. sugar. Put everything but the sugar together, let set overnight, then bring slowly to a boil, cooking until the grapes are soft. Strain. Bring the liquid gently to a boil. Add the sugar all at once to the boiling liquid, reheat to a boil, and boil about 5 more minutes, or until the jelly tests. (To test jelly, dip a cold spoon into the simmering mixture, and then hold it over a saucer for a few seconds. When a *double bead* forms on the spoon's edge, the jelly is done.)

Fox or Wild Grape Jelly

Follow the directions on a box of pectin for Concord grape jelly, using any fragrant wild grape. The wild grapes have a wilder, tangier taste than tamed ones, and make a wonderful jelly.

Grape-Stuffed Chicken
(Serves two to four.)

This delicious, easy recipe is adapted from a Native American dish.

Wash a whole frying chicken, and salt it inside and out. Heat the oven to 350°F. Stuff the bird with grapes removed from the stems, and seeded if they have objectionable seeds. The grapes may be salted a little first and tossed with 1 or 2 minced cloves of garlic. Let the grapes spill out and surround the chicken. Bake for $1\frac{1}{2}$ hours at 350°F, uncovered. You can baste it with its own juices a couple of times if you like. Wiggle a leg to see if it is loose, which lets you know the chicken is done. Serve the chicken with rice, and spoon grapes and their juice over the rice.

▣ PEARS

Pears, many species and even more varieties of the *Pyrum* genus (from the Latin *pirum,* "pear"), are easily recognizable even to small children. Pears and apples are of the same species; botanists disagree on where to place many of them. Some apples contain the grit cells we associate with the texture of pears; some pears are subglobose, the shape of apples. Some apples are elongated like pears.

Pear trees, originally introduced to Europe from Eurasia, are spread by cultivation as well as by tossed-away pear cores. Often pear trees are found on abandoned homesites, for they are long-lived trees. I have found them near decaying cabins and on abandoned farms, as well as occasionally in the woods.

DESCRIPTION, HABITAT, AND SEASON

Pear trees are small to medium, with spinelets on the branches; slender, smooth, sharply serrated or roundly serrated leaves; and a beautiful white five-petaled spring blossom. The fruits of the many trees of this large genus range in color from yellow to green to red to brown, and vary enormously in size, flavor, and texture. In the wild, they sometimes cross with *Sorbus* (mountain ash). In short, there are seemingly endless varieties, many of which have not been identified.

Look for ripe fruit from midsummer to early fall. Pears ripen more quickly on the tree and ground than any other large fruit I know, so they bear watching and picking at just the right moment.

HISTORY AND LORE

The Romans first introduced pears to Britain, where the Christian monks later tended to them. A legend has it that evil King John I of England was killed in 1216 by the monks of Swinsted, who were clever enough to put poison into a dish of pears so delicious as to overpower the taste of the poison.

R E C I P E S

In 1846, a Boston naturalist wrote that there were over 200 American varieties of pears, but that only about 20 of them were edible. That's about my experience with pears, but a friend tells me it's because I don't pick them right. So here is the right way: Pick pears while they are still hard, noting where you found the tree. Wrap them in a paper bag or cotton cloths and set them in the dark for up to 2 weeks, checking them daily so that when they are ripe, you will know. If you can find one abandoned pear tree with good pears, that's all you need: You can return to it year after year.

Lizzie's Pear and Ginger Preserves

Gather 1 quart chopped ripe pears; half a lemon, sliced thin, the seeds removed; about 2 cups sugar; 1 cup water; and ½ cup chopped candied ginger. You can add half a vanilla bean also. Bring to a boil, then simmer this mixture on low heat until the pears are transparent, and the syrup somewhat thickened. Stir it every few minutes. This makes a gorgeous, dark gold condiment that is fine on pound cake or ice cream.

▨ PLUMS

Prunus is the name of the genus that includes plums. The word *prunus* in Latin means "plum tree," though today we know prunes (dried plums) better than the fresh variety. Plums are small trees or shrubs of temperate North America and South America that bear fruit in late summer.

DESCRIPTION, HABITAT, AND SEASON

Plums are deciduous trees, the leaves serrated and alternate, oval to rounded, and smooth, with five-petaled flowers that bloom white or pink in spring. Many wild varieties of plums grow in the temperate parts of this country, with fruits green, golden, purple, blue, or red,

Pomological Magazine in 1835 reported that a plum tree, purchased sometime in the 1790s, would not bear, though it appeared healthy. Seven years later, during a violent thunderstorm, the tree was struck by lightning and destroyed. But afterward, the root put up a number of vigorous shoots, which grew into trees and subsequently produced much fine fruit. (In contemplating this story, I wonder if the tree needed male and female both to bear, and had no companions until the small trees came up.)

sometimes sweet, sometimes sour, sometimes clingstone, sometimes freestone, ripening in the fall. All are smooth skinned, some have a dusty "bloom" to the skin, and they usually have the characteristic of tasting sweet near the skin and sour near the stone. The fruits of all plums have a single flat stone, are usually over an inch in diameter, and are oval, with the faint or deep suggestion of a long indentation (called a suture) on one side.

The fruits of wild plums are smaller than commercial plums, often not more than an inch or so in diameter.

Among the best plums are several varieties of a beach plum, *Prunus maritima*, typical in shape, but variable in size and color, from lemon yellow through red to deep purple, from half an inch to two inches, that grows many places along the Atlantic Coast from Maine to North Carolina. It's tart, and makes a distinctive jam.

HISTORY AND LORE

Plums entered Britain from Asia originally, and are popular around the Mediterranean.

Plum bark is astringent, and has been used as a substitute for quinine in the treatment of malaria. The Indians used plums as laxatives, and claimed that in years when the plums were plentiful, dysentery abounded.

The fruit has been used for generations in Appalachia to make a sweet wine, as well as damson preserves. (The name damson indicates that the plum originated in Damascus.) One kind of wild American plum, the sloe, was used as a flavoring for homemade gin during the Depression, and sloe gin is still popular in some rural areas of the South. Its name comes from an Old English term for plum, *slah*.

R E C I P E S

One word of warning: The pits of all *Prunus* and *Malus* species (apples, peaches, plums, cherries) contain cyanide (cyanogenic glycosides) in such quantities that 12 pits or ½ cup of apple seeds contains a sufficient amount to kill an adult. So be careful about not letting seeds into the final food.

Plum Jam

Use any damson, greengage, mirabelle, Italian, or tasty wild plums. Wash, halve (but don't peel), and remove the pits from the wild plums, up to 1 quart, add an equal amount of sugar, and let the mix stand several hours before cooking. Then bring the pot to a boil and turn it down to a simmer. Stir often, cooking slowly until the syrup and fruit are thick and fragrant. Be careful not to scorch the jam. This usually takes under 1 hour, but does need constant attention.

▣ QUINCES

Quince trees are various species of the *Cydonia* genus. Modern shrub books sometimes call the genus *Chaenomeles*, or *Pseudocydonia*. Common species include *C. oblonga, C. maliformis* (also known as *C. vulgaris*) and *C. sinensis*. Some botanists place the quince in the *Malus* genus along with apples. Both quinces and apples are in the *Rosaceae* family, and quinces have the same internal aspect as apples; that is, a cartilage protects the seeds, carried in the center. *Cydonia* is the Latin name for the fruit and tree. *Oblonga* describes an oblong fruit shape, *maliformis* indicates a lopsided applelike fruit, and *sinensis* points to a Chinese origin. The genus is probably named for the ancient city of Cydon, on Crete. But another possibility is that the name, from *cy,* meaning "circular," and *donia,* a "gift," kin to our word *donate,* implies that quinces are "circular gifts." The Portuguese word for quince, *marmelo,* gives us our word *marmalade.* Most quinces found in America originated in the Orient.

DESCRIPTION, HABITAT, AND SEASON

Quinces grow on hardy, deciduous, small, thorny trees or shrubs with crooked branches. They have oval leaves similar to apple tree leaves, and beautiful red, pink, or rose flowers in early spring. They are found in the wild and cultivated in gardens and hedges. The fruit turns from pale green to pale yellow as it ripens, often has rosy cheeks, and is speckled with small dots that are actually glands. It looks like a little apple one to two and one-half inches in diameter, or an oblong up to five inches long. Many of the fruits will be lopsided. Quinces ripen in late fall, giving off an intense fruity perfume. Quinces grow well throughout the South and the mid-Atlantic states, and can tolerate winters as far north as Michigan. As the tree has dense growth and fairly nasty thorns, it forms an effective barrier. The sour quince makes wonderful jelly or marmalade. The Portuguese quince turns wine-red when cooked.

Today, the quince is out of fashion, but even fifty years ago, it was popular. My grandparents had a vigorous quince hedge between their long cinder driveway and their deep front yard. In the spring, the intense rosy blossoms were a joy, and in the fall, we always made quince marmalade to give neighbors at Christmas. As soon as the buds swelled in early spring, quince branches were brought into the house and forced (watered until they opened in the indoor heat), and that meant spring was under way.

HISTORY AND LORE

Quinces were known in ancient times as golden apples. The ancients loved the quince, believing it to be the fruit of happiness and love. In Paphos and Cyprus, temples to Venus were decorated with quinces. The ancient writer Goropius declared that the quince was the Golden Apple of the Hesperides. Pliny advised the quince as a remedy for swollen spleen and dropsy, and wrote that it alleviated pulmonary difficulties and allayed nausea. Quince flowers were made into a decoction for tired or sore eyes, and the fruit was a remedy for asthma. It was introduced by the Romans into Britain, where it was grown for a wine that was also supposed to cure asthma. It is still a popular fruit in Italy, often hybridized. Though some modern "designer" quinces have orange or red fruit, Sardinian quince trees have fruits weighing up to three pounds each, and Mulvian quinces are sweet enough to eat raw, these are rarities; wild American quinces for the most part are green-yellow, small, and sour.

Hildegard von Bingen, who reviled peaches and strawberries, adored the quince, and claimed that it cured rheumatism in an hour, and purged and decontaminated the body so that no healthy person who ate it would ever get arthritis or rheumatism.

Early American settlers also believed that quince juice overcame nausea. The juice of raw quinces, which is quite styptic—that is, it makes the mouth pucker—was used to subdue hemorrhage. The Indians also used the quince in conjunction with tobacco as an asthma cure. In the nineteenth century, quince marmalade was much prized. Quince blossom honey is a specialty today in some parts of the South.

R E C I P E S

Wild quinces are sour and unpleasant raw, not fit for eating, but after their autumn ripening they smell wonderful and can be used to make a delicious tart jelly. Quinces can also be stewed into a sauce resembling applesauce, or used as pie filling.

Quince Marmalade

Slice, but do not peel, ripe quinces—which will have paled to yellow, perhaps become tinged with red, but will remain hard. Measure them. In a steel or enamel pot, put the quinces and barely cover them with water. For every quart of quinces, add the juice and thinly sliced rind of 1 lemon. Bring to a boil, add an amount of sugar equal to that of quinces, and boil for 15 minutes, stirring gently but continuously. After that, raise the heat, and cook another 15 minutes, stirring constantly to prevent scorching. Put three or four saucers briefly in the freezer. When a blob of the marmalade holds a shape on a cold plate, it is ready. Jar and seal it. Feeling that the pale yellow-gray color of the marmalade was not very attractive, we'd add at the end 1 drop red food coloring. But do so carefully, only a tiny drop at a time, until the marmalade is a blushing pink. You could, instead, add a little bit of purple grape juice or a little red wine, toward the end of the cooking process, to achieve the same blush.

◼ STRAWBERRIES

Strawberries are probably America's favorite berry. The name of the American wild strawberry is *Fragaria virginiana*, apparently suggesting its fragrance and the fact that it was first identified in Virginia. (There are others in Europe and England, including a white one in the Alps.) Wild strawberries are found everywhere in the temperate United States, and grown commercially from North Carolina to Florida, and on the West Coast. Their common name is shrouded in mystery: Maybe they were called stray-berries after their meandering habit; perhaps straw-berries because straw was often laid beneath the heavy, ripening berries to prevent their sinking into the mud underneath them; some even think the habit of selling them strung on straws in medieval markets gave them their name.

DESCRIPTION, HABITAT, AND SEASON

Strawberries grow low to the ground beneath their bright green foliage. They have white blossoms and mother plants that put out runners to form new plants. They sport three leaflets on a divided leaf, and the berries (accessory fruits, really) are born singly and terminally. You will find the ripe fruit a month after the roselike blossoms appear in mid-May, though blossom and fruit may be found together. Although wild strawberries grow potentially everywhere, they prefer full sun, and sandy roadsides, hilltops, pastures, and upland meadows. Early summer is the time to begin looking for the tiny wild strawberries that were, according to the account of an early Virginia settler, so thick in some places that the white feet of cows were stained red as they grazed.

> The strawberye is the wonder of all the Fruites growing naturally in these partes . . .
>
> —Sir Walter Raleigh

Wild strawberries are so tiny that collecting them seems nearly futile, but they are wonderful. The best patch I ever found was by accident when I was cutting across an open field at the top of a hill, in search of a horse. I came back later and gathered a quart of wild strawberries, which for me was surely a record.

There is one strawberry imitator, the *Duchesnea indica,* or Indian strawberry. It is harmless but not good to eat. People are often fooled by this Indian strawberry, or snakeberry, which looks like the wild strawberry, leaves, fruit, and all, and has made its way around the world. Its flowers are yellow instead of white, but by the time of fruiting, the flowers have vanished, leaving behind only the clever impostors.

HISTORY AND LORE

In medieval art, strawberries are associated with the Virgin Mary. Early American chroniclers described "Indian strawberry" bread, a mixture of cornmeal and the mashed fruit baked in flat cakes in the coals of a fire. In colonial times, strawberries were eaten in great quantity as a cure for consumption (tuberculosis). Some recorded and believed that actual cures occurred. The famous eighteenth-century American diarist William Byrd II ate asparagus and strawberries every day that he could obtain them.

Strawberry shortcake has long been the dessert associated with Independence Day in the United States, for early July is generally when strawberries are ripe throughout the mid-Atlantic states.

Strawberry ice cream still runs a close third after vanilla and chocolate in the hearts of Americans, even with such beguiling competitive flavors as Ben & Jerry's Coffee Toffee Crunch.

R E C I P E S

Wild strawberries are by any economic measure a waste of time, for they are tiny and hard to pick. But they are worth a great deal in superior flavor and pleasure. Gathering these tiny fruits, most of the time no larger than the end of your little finger, is a labor of patient love, as you sit on the ground staining your jeans beyond recovery in an aura of strawberry essence. Ideally, they should be gathered in a flat, wide-bottomed basket, so they don't crush each other. But the reward is a flavor so intense it seems fair to say that each tiny wild berry concentrates more flavor than is found in five of the giant modern hybrids. When you get home, red fingered and sunburned, you would be wise to scrub with coarse soap, rinse, scrub again, and rinse, to exorcise possible chiggers and poison ivy. Then spend a few more hours picking out stems and caps. You really can't wash wild strawberries, they're so tiny. Just pick them carefully.

Wild Strawberry Jam

(This works well with commercial strawberries, blueberries, and blackberries, too. It makes a wonderful, fresh-tasting, runny jam.)

Take a quantity of wild strawberries, and add three-quarters as much sugar. Boil them gently together for 17 minutes without stirring, squeeze the juice of half a lemon over them, stir briefly, and seal them at once in sterilized jelly jars.

Fresh Berries for Winter

This method saves fresh fruit for out-of-season treats. The disadvantage is in the amount of sugar needed. Mix fresh, cleaned, slightly crushed berries with twice as much sugar (that is, 2 cups sugar to every 1 cup berries), stirring hourly until the sugar is dissolved. (If you don't, it may recrystallize in the jar.) Then store in sterilized jars tightly closed. The sugar preserves the fruit in its uncooked state. I've used it with mixed success, best with strawberries, but with freezers I'd choose another method of saving fresh fruit; that is, light sugaring and freezing.

Strawberry Soufflé

This is adapted from a famous Swiss hotel's recipe. It serves four, and can be doubled. Have all ingredients at room temperature.

I use four individual casseroles, and a large (10" × 13" or larger) 2"-deep baking dish half full of boiling water. Assemble 2 cups fresh wild strawberries, 1 lemon, ¾ cup powdered sugar, 4 large eggs, an 8-oz. block cream cheese, ½ cup granulated sugar, 4 Tbsp. of either rum, brandy, kirsch, or a mix, and 2 tsp. vanilla. First, clean and mash the 2 cups berries. Grate 1 Tbsp. lemon peel and set aside, then squeeze and strain the juice from the lemon. Add ½ cup of the powdered sugar and the lemon juice to the berries, stir well, and set aside. Separate the 4 large eggs; soften the 8-oz block of cream cheese; and measure the ½ cup granulated sugar into one cup and the liquor into another.

Preheat oven to 425°F. Butter four individual baking dishes or one large baking casserole, and dust with some of the granulated sugar. Save the rest. Beat egg yolks and cream cheese with the remaining 4 Tbsp. powdered sugar and the 2 tsp. vanilla for 5 minutes, then beat in the liquor and the lemon peel.

Beat egg whites with the granulated sugar until they hold soft peaks. Fold a blob of the whites into the yolk mixture, then pour the lightened yolks into the whites and fold. Divide the mixture among the casseroles, and set casseroles into the baking pan half full of boiling water. Bake about 20 minutes for the small soufflés, 40 minutes if using one large casserole.

When the hot soufflés are ready, pour the crushed berries over them and serve at once.

Strawberry Shortcake
(Serves four.)

I make this all the time, but it is especially good with wild strawberries. It can also be made with raspberries and blueberries. I think the oil is the secret. Or maybe it's the vanilla. Heat the oven to 400°F. Mix 1 package (2 cups) biscuit mix with 3 Tbsp. sugar and 3 Tbsp. cooking oil, then add ½ cup milk and ½ tsp. vanilla. Mix lightly. Handling as little as possible, pat the mixture out evenly on the bottom of an 8" or 9" cake pan that has been sprayed or oiled. Prick all over with a fork and bake until golden, about 10 to 15 minutes.

Cool. Split as you would a big biscuit. When you are nearly ready to serve dessert, whip 1 cup heavy cream with 2 Tbsp. sugar, a few grains salt, and 1 tsp. or so vanilla. Withholding 1 perfect berry for the top, crush 1 quart ripe berries over the bottom half of the shortbread and let some fall to the sides. Put the top half on, and pour any leftover syrup over it all. Top the whole with the whipped cream, and put the single beautiful berry in the middle. Let it sit 5 minutes before serving it. Cut into quarters.

Berry Vinegar

Pick over 2 pints of the fruit you are going to use to flavor the vinegar: raspberries, blackberries, strawberries, elderberries, gooseberries, etc. Place them in a crockery jug or jar, and pour over them 2 quarts good cider vinegar. After a day, pour the whole thing into a cheesecloth bag and let it drip until no more juice comes out. Save the liquid, throw away the fruit pulp, clean the earthen jug or jar thoroughly with hot water and soap, and repeat the process, using 2 more pints of the same fruit. Do this 3 or 4 times over 3 or 4 days for a strong-flavored vinegar, being careful to wash out the crock thoroughly between each day's new fruit.

FLOWERS
& HERBS

What are all the oranges imported into England to the hips and haws in her hedges?

—Henry David Thoreau

L est you think herb lore merely a quaint and primitive Appalachian pastime, it was estimated by the World Health Organization as late as 1985 that over 75 percent of the world's population depended upon plants (which are called herbs if they are used medicinally) as their *only* medicine. Herbing is not considered a dignified profession any longer, but medicinal herbs are still big business. And late in the eighties, *The Economic Botany Journal* reported that "America exports around 600 million dollars' worth of herbs annually, and imports ten to twenty million dollars' worth." Of this huge quantity of American medical plants, 90 percent or more are from the wild.

When you set out to pick herbs or flowers, you need scissors, a basket for gathering, and a field guide or two for identification of plants.

Know what you're doing before you add anything to your salad. You don't want to get a mouthful of poison ivy leaves or butter-cups—they are poisonous—by mistake.

▣ ROSE HIPS

Roses, members of the *Rosa* genus, come in thousands of varieties that include tea roses, bush roses, climbing roses, and wild roses. They are prized for their fragrance, and symbolize love in many cultures. Everyone knows what roses look like, and how wonderful they smell; but few have been intrepid enough to eat roses.

DESCRIPTION, HABITAT, AND SEASON

Roses are, of course, various members of the family *Rosaceae*, and borne terminally on the stems of the thorny shrubs. Roses can be from a foot tall to ten feet or so for climbers. All roses have dark green, smooth, serrated, opposite leaves, with a terminal leaf, usually five to seven leaflets on each stem.

Rose hips are the fruits of rosebushes, all rosebushes wild and tame have them, and they ripen in autumn, and are used after the first frost. Hips are a nickname of the hypanthia, or enlarged tori, the flower receptacles below the flower calyx, or seed container. The hips, also sometimes called haws, vary greatly in size and color, from the size of a huckleberry to the size of a small plum, and from light orange to deep scarlet. Few people know the great health secret of rose fruits. Rose hips have a high vitamin C content, about forty times as much as oranges, which I take to mean that there is a full day's requirement in one large rose hip.

HISTORY AND LORE

Rose hips appear in all sorts of herbal medicines and teas, touted for their excellent antiscorbutic quality. In the lean years of World War II, when citrus fruits were unobtainable, most people in northern Europe and Great Britain ate rose hips as an acceptable substitute for fresh fruits and vegetables. The darker the rose, the more flavorful the hip, goes one old saw. Even the flowers have value beyond their odor and lovely appearance. Crushed rose petals infused in water have long been a remedy for sore eyes.

RECIPES

Hips can be gathered from any rosebush, wild or cultivated. Collect them after the first frost, which softens their texture and their sour taste. (In England I have eaten hips that actually tasted sweet, but generally they are quite sour.) They have a high pectin content, and make nice sunset-colored jellies and syrups. These berrylike fruits are easy to see on a tramp across freeze-dried monotone autumn fields, or in some winter garden where almost everything else is asleep. *Rosa rugosa*, the "rugged rose," has an especially large, succulent hip, as does *R. canina* ("dog rose"), but all rose hips are usable. Many are sour, and all are seedy, so you probably wouldn't want to toss them in a salad.

Rose Hip Jelly

Assemble 4 cups rose hips, 6 green apples, chopped coarsely, 1 lemon, 6 cloves, half a cinnamon stick, 1 cup water, 1 box dried pectin, and 4 cups sugar. Cook everything but the pectin and sugar until tender. Mash the fruit mixture slightly. Cool, and strain the mixture through several layers of cheesecloth. If the liquid does not measure 4 cups, pour a little water through the dregs to make 4 cups. Mix liquid and pectin and bring to a boil, stirring all the while. When it boils vigorously, add the sugar all at once, and, stirring constantly, bring it to a boil again and boil 60 seconds. Remove from the stove, skim, and jar. This makes a pretty pink to red jelly that makes great Christmas presents, and is good for you.

Rose Hips for Winter

Collect some rose hips, at least 2 cups. Use an enamel or stainless steel pan. Add half as much water as you have rose hips. Cook the hips until they are tender. Mash them, and force them through a fine strainer. To this puree, add an equal amount of sugar, and boil the mixture gently only until the sugar is dissolved. Store in the refrigerator or freezer, and eat a spoonful a day for vitamin C, or enjoy the delicious conserve on your toast or pancakes.

Candied Rosebuds

Choose perfect, tiny buds of wild rose, fairy rose, or others, in the spring and summer. Tight, tiny buds hold together best, and you can also use larger buds, up to ¾" across. Boil them gently in a half-water, half-sugar mixture for about ½ hour, or until they begin to look chinalike, or semitransparent. Lift them carefully out of the syrup, and drain them on waxed paper. When they are well drained, roll them in granulated sugar, dry them thoroughly for 1 or 2 days in a dry, warm place, lay them carefully in a box, and seal them against moisture. Decorate cakes, cookies, or candies with them.

▩ VIOLETS

Viola species are numerous, the name meaning "violets" in Latin. They include pansies as well as violets.

DESCRIPTION, HABITAT, AND SEASON

Most people are familiar with the shy-nodding, small white, lavender, or purple long-stemmed violets that grow in lawns and gardens from early until late spring. They can be found in damp areas in the Temperate Zone east of the desert, in the continental United States. They have large, dark green, heart-shaped leaves, and are ubiquitous to shady areas and the edges of streams, as well as lawns, woods, and less well-kept yards. They have the reputation for sweetness, and bloom early in spring. We all know them, but few know that they are edible and pleasant.

HISTORY AND LORE

Ever since Diana changed Ia into a violet, to hide her from Apollo's unwanted ardors, violets have been the emblem of modesty, and the model of shyness. There are two interesting facts about violets: They are nature's litmus, and turn red in the presence of acid, and yellow in the presence of alkali. The other fact is that some violets smell divine, while others have little or no odor. This is apparently because the English violet *(V. odorata)*, grown by early settlers for perfume and medicine, and still popular as a scent, escaped from colonial gardens and intermingled with scentless native violets, thus causing a mixed population, in which some of the natives exude perfume, while identical others, untouched by the fragrant foreigner, don't have any odor at all.

RECIPES

It is still fashionable in France to decorate fancy cakes with candied violets. These delicate flowers tend to lose their shape with cooking, though they are preserved by the syrup. Violet leaves as well as flowers are nice in a green spring salad, for looks as well as for a shot of vitamin C.

Candied Violets

Violets may be prepared the same way as rosebuds, only cooked for much less time (around 10 minutes), and handled carefully. However, there is another way to "candy" rosebuds and violets. Wash and drain dry violets or the buds of wild roses. Dip into a wash of 1 egg white beaten thoroughly with 1 Tbsp. water, then shake gently in a bowl of sugar to cover each flower with sugar completely. Lay the flowers, not touching each other, on a cookie sheet, and dry in the oven at the lowest possible heat setting until each flower is completely dry. Handling the flowers carefully, store them in an airtight container, and use them to decorate cakes.

▣ MINT

Some kind of wild mint (*Mentha spp.*) grows near you. These plants are identifiable from their square stems and pungent odors. We find the plant's name in our word *menthol*. There are several dozen mints that grow wild in this country, as well as many cultivars that combine flavors nicely, but

Peppermint

A BRIEF HISTORY OF THE MINT JULEP

In colonial times, liquor was considered safer than water to drink. After all, back in Europe, water was the most dangerous drink of all. Alcoholic beverages, on the other hand, insulated pioneers from cold, slaked the thirsts brought on by salted meats, and anesthetized folks against the miseries of colonial living.

The happy discovery around 1800 that excellent whiskey could be made from maize created a nation of bourbon devotees. When George Washington ran for legislature in 1758, he doled out a quart and a half of liquor for every voter. When we won independence and George Washington's brand-new government tried to raise money by imposing a tax on whiskey, they were faced with the famous Whiskey Rebellion, resulting in our first civil bloodshed as a nation. Although the insurrection was quickly quelled, many farmer-distillers, deciding that facing Indians was preferable to facing revenuers, moved westward specifically to be able to continue making untaxed whiskey.

A common breakfast item throughout the colonies north and south was a julap, a drink made of rum, brandy, or whiskey, mixed with sugar and water. Mint was soon added, probably functioning as a sort of night-breath cleanser. And thus the mint julep was born.

unfortunately will not persist in the wild. Some of the harsher mints, like menthol, would not be appealing for food, but all are safe to try, and many are delicious.

DESCRIPTION, HABITAT, AND SEASON

Peppermint *(Mentha piperita)* ("peppery mint," from the hot flavor) and spearmint *(M. spicata)* (from the plant's spiky shape) are two favorites, and wherever one is found usually the other is also. All mints have square stems. Spearmint grows to about two feet, sometimes higher, each unbranching spear a solid emerald green color. The leaves are opposite, one to two inches long, serrated. The midsummer flowers are whitish to purple. Peppermint is similar but has wider and shorter leaves, is a slightly darker green, and the stalks have a purplish tinge. Both grow in early to midsummer, usually in huge patches. They are most obvious because of their sharp perfumes; the slightest disturbance, even brushing a leaf, causes it to give off its peppermint or spearmint aroma. The plants have disappeared by late August. Spearmint, peppermint, and other mints that look similar, grow in damp places, such as alongside creeks and rivers, in ditches by road-sides, and in low-lying pastures.

HISTORY AND LORE

Mint is the plant of virtue, named for a Greek nymph who had the bad luck to fall in love with Pluto, god of the underworld. When Persephone, the wife of Pluto, discovered that the brazen nymph had chosen to seduce her husband, she in a fit of jealousy turned the poor girl into a lowly mint plant.

Mint is said to have cured more than forty illnesses among early settlers here, from halitosis to high blood pressure. Today, 95 percent of its use is as flavoring for candy or toothpaste.

RECIPES

Mint Tea

I dry both spearmint and peppermint in my kitchen in summer in huge bunches, which makes the kitchen smell good, then strip the crisp leaves off into jars when they're dry, and use them all winter for a hot tea that is comforting, head clearing, and harmless. A handful of the dried leaves steeped 3 to 5 minutes in a teapot of water is all that's needed. Pour it out through a strainer for a delicate, pale tea.

Mint Jelly

The exact proportions of water and sugar are necessary to make this product jell. Use $4\frac{1}{2}$ cups water, 1 large bunch of spearmint, pepper-mint, or, better, mixed mints, 1 box pectin, $4\frac{1}{2}$ cups sugar, 1 Tbsp. cider vinegar, 1 drop blue food color (optional). Simmer the water with the bruised, cleaned mint leaves and stems for 15 minutes in a covered pot. Allow to cool entirely. Strain to remove stems and leaves. Mix pectin and mint water thoroughly, bring it to a boil, and add sugar all at once. Return to boil, boil 1 minute hard, remove from heat, skim. The resulting jelly is an unattractive pale yellow. Add vinegar, and food color if desired, and pour immediately into small jars. If you wish, you can add a perfect leaf or two of mint to each jar. When cool, pour melted paraffin over the tops to seal. This jelly is *the* accompaniment for roast lamb.

Mint Julep

Possibly the finest use to which bourbon whiskey can be put is in the mint julep. If you have the intent to get drunk, or only slightly loopy, this in my estimation is the way to do it. You can only do it in summer, when you've a great thirst, and the mint is fresh. There is a sterling silver container known as a julep cup, but any glass will do. Pick 2 stems of good mint about 8" long each. I personally prefer a curly English variety, mild and somewhere between peppermint and spearmint in flavor, but any will do. Wash the mint well. From 1 stalk, strip the leaves into your cup. Add 2 tsp. confectioners' sugar, and with a wooden knife handle, bruise the leaves with the sugar, grinding them together until the sugar is stained with mint, and the leaves are mashed and shredded. Next fill the glass with crushed ice, and pack it down. Now fill it to the top with bourbon whiskey, stir it well, "plant" the other stem down into the glass, and serve. (Some say add pineapple or cherries or orange slices or lemon, but Virginians and Kentuckians consider anything but mint a desecration.)

▧ CATNIP

Catnip's botanic name is *Nepeta cataria*. *Nepeta* comes from a Tuscan town, Nepet, but the word in Latin means "cat nip."

Description, Habitat, and Season

Catnip is a grayish green, slightly fuzzy-stemmed, erect mint (look for the square stem), one to four feet tall. It has white to pale lilac flowers that bloom in late summer to early fall, and the leaves are pointed. Though the odor is minty, it is distinctive.

Catnip grows all summer long, throughout the Temperate Zone, at the edges of woods, in fields and pastures, in roadside ditches, at the edges of country vegetable gardens, and can be gathered anytime during the summer months, given to your cats fresh, or hung in bunches from a rafter and dried for winter use.

History and Lore

Catnip, widely distributed throughout this country, has a long history as a soothing tea useful for comforting, and even curing, winter colds and summer heat stress. It has been found useful for stimulating sluggish appetites, and for lulling people into sound sleep. It also has a long history of inducing ecstasy and aggression in cats. They appear to love it, and be made drunk by it.

It is at least as much fun to watch cats playing with catnip as it must be for the cats to do it. Our cats rub their cheeks in it; they gnaw on it, they roll over in it, toss it into the air and let it fall on top of them, and then they get into drunken-but-desultory battles with the other cats. Eventually they go and sleep it off, and ignore catnip for a week or so. Of the fourteen cats I've owned as an adult, some of them living into their twenties, only two were unaffected by catnip.

Catnip is reputed, as it does to cats, to make timid people bold, and I've even read that hangmen several hundred years back would fortify themselves with catnip before doing business.

R E C I P E S

Catnip Mice
(For cats.)

You can stuff little scrap-cotton bags to make dried catnip toys for your favorite cats, who will love them for the smell, so the shape isn't important, though adding some sort of tail seems to enhance the cats' enjoyment. You can also give catnip to your cats fresh, and watch their ecstatic drunks. Our vet assures us it won't hurt the cats, and some people use it as a training device by putting it on the places where they prefer that the kitties sleep or play.

Catnip Tea
(For people.)

Crush a handful of catnip in your hand, and steep it in a pot of boiling water for 3 minutes, to yield a soothing and refreshing tea, said to calm the stomach and the nerves. Catnip can also be dried (hung upside down in bunches), the dried leaves stripped off the stem and stored in jars, for year-round tea. Many other fragrant herbs, like sage, basil, savory, rosemary, or thyme, may also be made into tea that is soothing and harmless. Either the fresh or the dried herbs can be used.

▣ NASTURTIUMS

Nasturtiums ("nose-twisters," from *nasus,* Latin for "nose," and *torquo,* Latin for "twist") are in the same family with watercress. Nasturtium is the common name. Its folk name is Indian cress; its scientific name is *Tropaeolum majus. Tropaeolum* derives from the Latin word *tropaeum,* or "trophy"; it describes how the leaves are shield shaped, and the flowers helmet shaped. White men first saw nasturtiums on the shores of South America.

DESCRIPTION, HABITAT, AND SEASON

The nasturtium, whose leaves are the same round shape as watercress leaves, is a native of Peru and Chile, where many colorful varieties thrive. Many varieties have escaped civilization and are found in the wild, in ditches, along roads, at the edges of pastures. They are lowly five-petaled, two-inch flowers with round leaves. Both the leaves (round and light green) and the many-colored scarlet, red, orange, or yellow flowers grow on spindly, wavy stalks or stems. They have a peppery taste (a cross between watercress and horseradish) and are wonderful additions to spring or summer salads.

HISTORY AND LORE

Elizabeth Christina, Linnaeus's daughter, observed that nasturtiums emitted a tiny spark from time to time, visible only in the dark. I knew of this from childhood, and used to sit and watch my mother's nasturtiums, hoping to catch sight of one. I never did. Nor have I ever seen a ghost, a UFO, or the green flash as the sun goes down, though I have spent many an hour looking.

These flowers are easy to find and to grow and add a cheerful and pleasant note to any flower garden. This pretty, long-blooming flower (spring to frost) has an antibiotic and antibacterial principle, and thus found use as a mild medicine among the South American Indians. It has been eaten since in Europe to treat genital and urinary infections. The flower buds and the mature seedpods make an exceptional substitute for capers.

R E C I P E S

Faux Capers

Bring to a boil a mix of one-quarter water and three-quarters cider vinegar, with a dash of salt. In a jar place a garlic clove and a handful of tight nasturtium buds, or, after the flowering, the seedpods, and pour the boiling pickling water over them. Seal and wait 2 weeks to use.

▨ MARIGOLDS

The Marigold (*Calendula officinalis*) is a bright yellow flower with a pungent fragrance that makes a nice bright yellow tea, and is otherwise a usefull plant medicinally. The name, kin to the word *calendar*, means "of the months," and probably indicates its long growing season. It is used to color cheese, as a tea, in salads, as a wool dye, a hair dye, and an ingredient in other cosmetic preparations.

DESCRIPTION, HABITAT, AND SEASON

The marigold is not native to this continent, but escaped from colonial gardens. It is found mostly in cultivated fields, in full sun, and is an all-summer bloomer with oval, pale green leaves and round, radiant, many-petaled flowers of bright yellow or gold.

HISTORY AND LORE

Medicinally, marigold is an anti-inflammatory, an antiseptic, and as such is used in soothing eyedrops and for treatment of external ulcers on the skin.

RECIPES

In a Japanese restaurant, I once ordered marigold tea, and got three yellow marigold flower heads floating in scalding water. To my surprise, it tasted really good. Marigold tea, I later learned, is said to promote menstruation, and to be sedative in an infusion.

Flower Teas

Gather the full-blooming flower heads of jasmine, violets, lavender, marigolds, or honeysuckle, or the petals of fragrant roses, and steep them 3–5 minutes in boiling water, or dry them carefully for later use, and store them loosely in jars. I have in the attic a screen door on two sawhorses, which makes a nearly perfect place for drying herbs and flowers.

NUTS

The bitter-sweet of a white-oak acorn which you nibble in a bleak November walk over the tawny earth is more to me than a slice of imported pine-apple.

—Henry David Thoreau

When you focus on wild foods, you discover a lot that other people just don't notice. For instance, one day you'll stumble on the fact that a lot of people have black walnut trees in their yards, and rake up and throw away bushels of the intense, oily-flavored nuts. You might want to try some.

There are many varieties of hickory nuts in this country, widely scattered throughout the temperate parts of the United States, and some are excellent. I've gathered wild pecans in Georgia, smaller than the ones you can buy at Christmas in the stores, but just as good. I've found beechnuts in Missouri.

I truly love those times, during brisk fall, for that is when the nuts fall, when I can walk through the speckled or washed woods, freed from the annoyance of insects and reptile-wariness, tramping on and through the incredible colors that nature paints itself with in autumn, feeling the heat of the waning sun on my head when the wind is still, feeling the chill of coming winter when the wind takes up—and nutting. I look forward, too, to coming home and making a fresh pot of tea or coffee, sitting down with my husband or a friend or one of the children. I'll assemble the equipment for our surgery, a couple of industrial-strength hammers, an old brick to hit the nuts on, a heavy plastic bag to put the nuts in for the first shattering (to keep the pieces of shell from flying into the far corners of the kitchen or into anyone's eyes), crackers, and picks. It is then that we can get into real philosophy: where did a word come from? what do you think about UFO abductions? capital punishment? what *really* causes cancer? and it is then that the memories of my grandfather Andaddy come back to me.

You know the term "a spell" in southern dialect? "Sit a spell," they used to say to me, those old ladies on our street, the men in country stores, my friends' grandfathers, and my grandfather's friends. Part of it was that I made them nervous with my tireless energy, but part of it was they wanted to talk while they shelled peas, unstrung beans, or shattered and picked walnuts. "Sit a spell" promised a discourse on the ways of the lightning blinking up a storm, and why thunderstorms occurred either in the late afternoon or at night, hardly ever in the morning, or what it meant when the cows on a hill all stood facing the same way: Maybe rain was coming, maybe fish were biting. "Here, honey," one might say, handing me a walnut meat that was entire. "Don't say I never gave you anything," the giver would warn.

Sometimes they'd bring the War into the discussion, usually concerning the picture in a local paper of one of the hometown boys in England or Germany or on one of those islands, sometimes even Daddy.

"Here, honey," someone would say. "Snaps these beans for me." They speculated on whether they'd ever find gold, or tin, or iron, or cassiterite in

the nearby mountains, or if it was all mined out. Was it true that you had to near kill a walnut tree for it to bear good nuts? Andaddy would nod sagely: The one in our drive had been hit many times by his confounded machine, the Model T he was so proud of. Got hit by lightning a lot, too. He'd thought it was dead. Then it started giving the biggest and best black walnuts in town. So you never could tell.

More cracking. More hammering. More tasting. The cost of walnuts if you were to find them in the store.

The cost of everything!

Well, if I had money, reckon I'd just drink it away, someone would say. Laughter all around.

Black Walnut

🔲 BLACK WALNUTS AND BUTTERNUTS

Black walnuts and butternuts are two species of the *Juglans* genus, and the nuts of both taste similar. The name of the walnut family explains how highly regarded it was once: *Juglans* means in Latin the penis

head of Jupiter—which one assumes
implies fairly high praise
for this nut.

DESCRIPTION,
HABITAT, AND
SEASON

The leaves of both kinds
of walnuts are alternate,
once-compounded, with
seven to seventeen pairs
of light green, serrated,
fragrant leaves (and no tip
leaflet), so that the visual effect
from a distance is lacy or ferny.

Butternut

Black walnut trees grow all over our
town, and all over our woods, as do, to a lesser
extent, a related species called butternuts. The black walnut trees
have long been prized for their wood, and their solidity, their regal
shapes and pretty light foliage. They grow to 150 feet, have an aro-
matic odor that most find pleasant, and a deeply furrowed, dark gray
or blackish bark.

Butternut trees, sometimes called white walnuts, are similar trees,
but the fruits are more elongated than the green fruits of the walnut,
and the trees have lighter gray bark that is not as tightly furrowed.
The nuts taste the same to me. Walnuts are the strongest-flavored of
our wild nuts.

In recent years, however, when gardening has become something
of a national obsession, folks sometimes want to be rid of their
walnut trees, for the *Juglans* species exude an unfriendly substance
called juglone (after the plant) into the soil that keeps a lot of things
from growing near it. It's actually an adaptive mechanism of the tree,
which naturally is trying to get all the nearby soil nutrients for itself.

HISTORY AND LORE

I have read that walnut trees can be tapped for a sap that makes a syrup similar to maple, but I have not tried it. It must be made in the early spring, when the sap rises in all trees. (See the section on "Maple Syrup," pages 161–62.)

Despite vegetable gardeners' dislike for walnut trees, they are beautiful and formidable plants, and a lot of them still reign high over backyards, casting light shade on the ground below. In autumn they drop fragrant green fruits that are ripened nuts encased in protective coverings. Left around the yard, the fruits turn black and mushy. The best way to shuck the walnuts down to the shell is to dump a bushel of the nuts into the street or driveway, and drive over them for a week or so, which will take off the husks. Wear gloves when you handle walnuts of any sort, or your hands will get stained yellow-brown, and the stain will stay literally until you grow entirely new skin.

R E C I P E S

The nuts of either the walnut or the butternut, when ripe and unhusked, are hard, and have to be broken open with a vise or hammer, and the heavenly oily nut meats removed with little picks. It's a job to be done while drinking tea and passing time with people you love talking to when you haven't anything pressing to do. Be careful not to let any pieces of shell into the nut meats, or you will have a broken tooth somewhere around the table: They are that hard.

And when you're done, here is how to use the nut meats.

Walnut or Butternut Torte

Heat the oven to 350°F, and assemble 10 eggs, 1⅓ cups sugar, 1 Tbsp. vanilla, 1 to 2 cups black walnut or butternut meats, salt, cinnamon, allspice, ¼ cup sifted flour, 2 cups cream, 6 Tbsp. powdered sugar, and 1 Tbsp. instant coffee dissolved in 2 Tbsp. rum or brandy with ½ tsp. vanilla added.

Separate the 10 eggs carefully. Beat the sugar with the yolks, and add the 1 Tbsp. pure vanilla, the nut meats finely ground in the blender, and a pinch each of salt, cinnamon, and allspice, and mix thoroughly. Beat the egg whites until stiff, sprinkle with the sifted flour, and gently fold in the flour and the yolk mixture. Bake in three well-oiled cake pans until done, about 20 to 30 minutes. Turn out the cooled cakes onto waxed paper. Whip the cream with the powdered sugar and the coffee-rum-vanilla mixture. Ice between the layers and on top. If desired, you may sprinkle the top with more walnut meats. I don't know anyone with the strength to do this more than once a year, but it's ambrosial.

Pickled Green Walnuts

Pick 50 small green walnuts (black or butternut) off the tree around the first of June when they are hard, green, and small. They must be used before the shell develops inside. Don't shell them or husk them. Run a hatpin or fork through them, and don't use any that the pin won't pierce. (They expel a sap or liquid at the first prick, sometimes shooting it 2 feet or more.) Prick each walnut several times. Scald them in boiling water, drain them, then stir enough salt into water that an egg will float on it. Immerse the walnuts in the brine for 3 days, change the brine, leave 3 more days, change the brine, and leave 1 week, keeping them weighted and covered. After the 2 weeks is over, drain, rinse, and pat dry the walnuts. Let them sit in the sun for a day to dry entirely. They will become jet black. Pierce again several times with a needle. Make the pickling mixture: 2 thumbs of gingerroot, sliced, a handful of whole peppercorns, a handful of whole allspice, a handful of whole cloves (one method says to remove the clove heads), a handful of mustard seed, and 1 or 2 grated nutmegs. Bring to a boil the spices and enough vinegar to cover the walnuts, and boil for 5 minutes. Cover the walnuts with the boiling vinegar, cover tightly, and let them age for 1 month or more. They will last 5 years. Note: These were considered a great delicacy a century ago; I have made them only once, and did not find them very good. They were spicy, but also very salty and styptic. The method is the same in all three old cookbooks where I have found a recipe for them. It occurs to me that green English walnuts would make a much better product, but they don't grow wild in America.

Pickled walnuts (which can also be purchased at specialty food shops) are an ingredient in the best sauce I ever tasted, alleged to have been invented at the Pendennis Club in Louisville, Kentucky, by a chef named Henry Bain, for whom the sauce is named. It is a hot, spicy concoction of a lumpy consistency, dark blackish brown in color. It contains many ingredients—all of them already themselves pre-pared—including Worcestershire sauce, steak sauce, catsup, anchovies, Tabasco sauce, and pickled walnuts. Henry Bain Sauce is absolutely delicious on steak or beef or with a cheese sandwich or nearly anything else I could name.

▓ HICKORY NUTS AND PECANS

There are many species of wild hick-ory nuts that grow throughout the Temperate Zone of the United States. Their genus is *Carya* (named for their characteristic opposite ser-rated leaves).

Hickory Nut

DESCRIPTION, HABITAT, AND SEASON

From a distance it is not easy to distinguish between hickory and walnut trees. Of course up close, the nuts tell you. Hickories have four-sectioned husks, nowhere near as thick as walnuts. Hickory trees can grow over a hundred feet tall. These trees have leaves similar to walnut trees, once-compounded, alternate, nine to seventeen leaflets. They grow in warmer parts of the Temperate Zone, and the nuts fall in autumn. Hickory nuts are pale tan, two opposite sides flattened, and two convex. They are about an inch long and across, and much milder-flavored than either white or black walnuts. The pecan, darker tan and somewhat elongated, is a thin-shelled hickory nut of the Deep South, especially Georgia and Mississippi. Some of the new, thin-shelled varieties of pecans have escaped into the wild, as have the smaller, harder-shelled, older varieties. The best of the hickories come from the shagbark hickory tree, recognizable by its long, loose, gray scaly bark. Some hickories are bitter, and one is called a mock nut, because the shell is so hard and the meat so nearly nonexistent that it mocks the forager. So, crack and taste one before you go to the trouble of collecting and shelling a bunch. But a good hickory is a delicious nut: mild and sweet, just like a pecan.

Pecan

◼ BEECHNUTS

Fagus is the Latin for "beech tree," and the name of the genus; the word *fagus* (from the Greek *phegos*, "edible") notifies us that the fruit of the tree is good food. Beech trees, *Fagus grandifolia* or *F. sylvatica*, grow anywhere in rich soil and sheltered locales east of the Mississippi River, and from Canada to southern Georgia.

Description, Habitat, and Season

The beech is a beautiful, tall (over a hundred feet) tree with smooth, roundish but triangular, tan nuts and a rich golden-red fall color to the leaves at the time the nuts are ripe. The tree has a smooth, pale, grayish bark, and long, coarsely serrated, oblong-ovate leaves that are blue-green on top, and

lighter green underneath. It is often planted by farsighted landowners for future shade. The tannish nuts, which mature in autumn, tend to fall out of the papery husks, which tend to stay on the tree, and you have to beat the squirrels to them. Beechnuts are darker in color and stronger-flavored than hickories, but not as strong-flavored as walnuts, and some are downright bitter.

R E C I P E S

Nut Pie

Preheat the oven to 350°F. Assemble 1 stick butter, 2 Tbsp. flour, 1 cup brown sugar, 1 cup white sugar, 2 tsp. vanilla extract, 2 eggs, and 1 cup shelled pecans, black or white walnuts, beechnuts, or hickory nuts. In a food processor, blend the butter, flour, sugars, vanilla, and eggs until light and smooth. Pour into an uncooked piecrust (see recipe on pages 180–81), sprinkle the nuts on top, and bake for 40 minutes or until puffed and browned and a knife in the middle comes out nearly clean.

▨ COCONUTS

Coconut palms (*Cocos* spp.), among the oldest plants on earth, grow along tropical and subtropical beaches, bearing coconuts free for the taking. Their name comes from a Spanish word, *coco*, that means "frown" or "grimace," because the inner hairy shell looks like an angry, scrunched-up face.

DESCRIPTION, HABITAT, AND SEASON

Coconut palms have the typical flat, evergreen leaf and rough, overlapped bark of palm trees everywhere, and they are frost sensitive. Of the many species, some coconut palms fruit year-round, some at specific times of the year. Their large green fruits—roughly a foot or more in diameter when ripe—are highly visible to anyone on the lookout. To tell if a coconut is ripe, shake it, and if you can hear water sloshing around inside, it's ready.

In this country, coconuts can be found in Florida, and sometimes in states as far north as South Carolina, all along the Gulf of Mexico coast, on the California coast, and throughout Hawaii.

Coconuts propagate by floating from place to place, taking root where they land, which is why they are found on all tropical coasts not only of America but also the rest of the world.

HISTORY AND LORE

Like the kernel of most nuts, the coconut meat is fatty and nutritious. It has found uses in cosmetics and in cooking, particularly in confections like cookies, where crispness is necessary. It is used in medicine and in industry. Copra, sun-dried coconut meat, was once the greatest export of the Hawaiian Islands.

R E C I P E S

If you find a coconut on the beach, shake it near your ear and listen for sloshing to determine if it is good to eat. Strip off the green outer husk (you need a heavy, sharp knife or machete), remove the fibrous inner layer, and crack the hard inside shell (which also calls for a serious hammer or machete). Inside that shell is the shell lining, or the meat, and in the center of it is a pearly, drinkable substance called coconut milk, which is sterile, and fine to drink straight from the coconut.

Coconut Custard Pie

Make a piecrust as directed on pages 180–81. Heat oven to 450°F. Scald 2 cups whole milk, but do not boil. Into a blender, break 4 large eggs. Add ¾ cup white sugar, a few grains salt, and 1 tsp. vanilla. Turn on the blender, and gradually pour the hot milk into the other ingredients. In a bowl, mix the custard with 2 cups grated coconut. Pour into pastry, place in oven on a cookie sheet, then reduce heat at once to 350°F, and bake for about 45 minutes, or until the top is nicely browned and the center is firm.

Unbelievably Easy Coconut Pie

Preheat oven to 325°F. Grease a heat-resistant glass pie pan. Mix together the following: 1 cup sugar, ¾ cup biscuit mix, ⅓ cup margarine, melted, 2 tsp. vanilla, 6 eggs, and ¾ cup milk. Pour them into the pie pan, top with 1 cup shredded coconut, and bake until done, about 1 hour.

Coconut Bacon

Here is another way to fix coconut that is so delicious you won't believe it isn't meat. Heat the oven to 300°F. Break the outer hairy brown shell of the coconut with a hammer. Discard the milk or save it for another use, and remove the flesh by wedging a knife tip between the shell and flesh, and popping it off. Leave on the brown skin of the white meat. Slice the meat into strips with a sharp blade, or on a slicer. Spread the strips on a cookie sheet, salt them lightly, then bake them slowly until they brown slightly. Check them often, and move them around so that they brown evenly.

Cooled, these crisp, toasted coconut strips are fine as a nibble. They are delicious eaten with cold soup. They make a wonderful condiment for a hot curry. They taste remarkably like bacon.

MISCELLANEOUS FORAGING

*We cultivate imported shrubs in our front yards for the beauty
of their berries, while at least equally beautiful berries grow
unregarded by us in the surrounding fields.*

—Henry David Thoreau

Wild foods are, of course, free for the picking. But so, quite frequently, are cultivated plants that no one else wants. Walking one day, you may discover, as I did, a row of flowering crab apple trees planted along a suburban street for the blossom and shade, but not for the fruit, and you'll notice how much good food is wasted. Almost every field has got horseradish growing in it, and almost nobody digs fresh horseradish anymore. Almost every town has its lanes of maple trees, which nobody outside of New England taps for the expensive, delicious syrup. Modern farmers who raise corn harvest it by machine, which leaves a lot of perfectly good ears just lying on the ground.

As mentioned, I have seen lambs'-quarters in city lots, and ripe blackberries growing in Central Park in New York City. At picnics, people gather up garbage bags full of watermelon rind to toss in the nearest Dumpster.

In every case there is free food nobody seems to want. The point is, if you look in the right places, and are willing put in the labor of preparation, you will be rewarded with good things to eat.

▣ INDIAN CORN

In 1961, my friends Julia and Jeanne and I made the grand tour of Europe, and by August we were driving through northern Italy, Liechtenstein, and Austria, when we noticed that we could never find corn on the menus of the places where we ate, though in the car we passed mile after mile of cornfields. Back in Virginia it was the season for sweet corn on the cob, and as we talked, we got hungrier and hungrier. As a consequence, when we stopped for lunch, after a small amount of soul searching, we helped ourselves to six ears of corn out of some farmer's field, planning to borrow a pot and cook it that night wherever we landed.

We pulled up at a house with a B&B sign, made arrangements to spend the night, and explained that we needed a pot to cook our corn in. Imagine our surprise when the woman said, in German, "You stole that."

Was she psychic? How did she know? We sheepishly confessed, explaining in horrible pidgin-German combined with horrible pidgin-English how homesick we were for corn. She shrugged, and gave us a pot. And stood, arms crossed, to watch what we would do next. In fact, another farm woman showed up soon after, and stood watching also. And another. None of them smiling. We brought a cup of water to the boil, and cheerfully put in the six ears, shucked, gorgeous and golden, and steamed them for the holy seven minutes. We took them out, gilded three with butter, and took a bite each. Well, we tried to take a bite. Puzzled, we opined they hadn't cooked long enough, so we returned them to the pot. After we had done that several times and an hour had passed and they still weren't edible, and the farm women had watched the entire operation solemnly (by then there were four of them in the kitchen leaning up against the wall to observe the insane and thieving Americans), it dawned on us that this wasn't our kind of corn. Europeans don't eat sweet corn, only cornmeal made from fodder corn. Those women kept straight faces the whole time, but every time I think of them I imagine them telling the story to someone, laughing so hard they are falling on the floor, whooping and slapping their knees at the stupidity of Americans.

Corn, a grass of unknown origin, is probably native to Central America, and was introduced to Europe first by Christopher Columbus, who called it *mahiz,* or "maize." Its scientific name is *Zea mays.* Corn, purchased or stolen from the Indians, sustained both the Jamestown colony in 1607 and the Plymouth colony in 1620, so it is fitting that *zea* in Greek means "I live." The word *corn* in Old English (Anglo-Saxon) meant a hard nub of something, such as a peppercorn, or a corn of salt (as in corned beef.) Corn came to mean whatever grain had hard "corns." Thus in England, the word *corn* came to mean wheat. From there it came, through the linguistic process known as generalization, to designate whatever the major grain of an area was: So in the case of the colonies, maize was soon called corn.

DESCRIPTION, HABITAT, AND SEASON

Corn is, of course, a tall, large cane grass six or more feet high that is cultivated throughout the eastern and middle sections of the continental United States. It has the flat, light green leaves typical of canes. It can be found north of the Tropics, from sea to shining sea.

HISTORY AND LORE

It has been said that, without Indian corn, hard corn, feed corn, America would never have been colonized and civilized. Wheat takes about six months to grow, but a corn crop matures in half that time, and some of it matures in six weeks. Unlike wheat, corn doesn't deteriorate when left in the field, but can be left on the stalk until the owner needs corn. Wheat, of course, must be harvested when it is ripe.

Corn's only fault is that it severely depletes the soil it grows in, so until crop rotation was discovered, wherever corn grew for two or three years, nothing else much would grow from then on. The American Indians were cleverer than the English settlers at this game: Some planted in each hill of corn a whole fish and a handful of wood ashes, which replenished the soil. Other Indians knew, too, that planting beans in the same hills with corn returned nitrates to the depleted soil, and in addition allowed the bean vines to use the cornstalks for climbers. The English, impatient with such foolishness, took a while to catch on that the Indians knew what they were doing.

Nowadays corn and other crops, such as soybeans, are rotated, or grown in the fields in alternate years, to replenish the soil. By the time Columbus first "discovered" corn, American Indians had already developed over three hundred different varieties that included many kinds of colored corn, hard corn (feed corn), popcorn, and sweet corn (corn that can be eaten off the cob).

R E C I P E S

Today, a harvesting machine often misses some ears of corn, leaving them still attached to the stalk, or lying on the ground still neatly wrapped in their husks. Only a few of these windfall ears collected on a chilly fall or winter afternoon will yield you a good supply of cornmeal. So collect 12 or so ears of hard corn (corn used to feed stock) left by the harvesters. (Soft corn, a marvel of cultivariation, will be readily distinguishable, for the kernels of it when old are soft and shrunken and moldy, whereas hard corn kernels are sturdy, and hard as rocks.) Take off the husks, dust the ear, and worry off the hard, dry grains of corn with your fingers (or hit or rub the ear against something to dislodge them). Grind about ½ cup of the kernels at a time in your blender until it becomes cornmeal, and store in small packages of 1 cup or so each in the freezer. (Each large ear averages 1 cup of meal.) This is whole grain cornmeal, and contains corn germ, corn oil, and corn bran, as well as carbohydrate. It is infinitely superior to any you can buy, *but must be frozen or it goes rancid quickly*. It makes wonderful corn bread and spoon bread.

Finally, this corn keeps naturally on the ear. I just ground an ear of red corn that's been hanging in my kitchen for several years, and made hoecakes (see method below), which were perfectly fresh tasting and delicious. Corn is truly an amazing grain.

Country Corn Bread

Preheat the oven to 375°F. Put a large iron skillet in the oven to heat. In your blender, put 1 egg, 1 cup and a slosh of milk, 1 tsp. baking soda, 1½ cups cornmeal, ½ cup biscuit mix or Baking Mix (see recipe on page 181), 1 tsp. sugar, 1 tsp. salt, and ¼ cup melted bacon drippings. Mix. Remove the skillet with an oven glove and put 1 Tbsp. bacon fat or other oil in it, tilt it around to grease the bottom, and pour in the batter. Return to the oven and bake about ½ hour, or until it's risen and begun to brown at the edges. Of course you can use margarine, or butter, or vegetable oil, and you can leave out the sugar (or put more in)—but it really does taste better with bacon fat.

Grand National Spoon Bread Champion

In 1975 *Commonwealth* magazine and the Virginia State Chamber of Commerce sponsored a national spoon bread contest. My spoon bread won first prize, and the title Grand National Spoon Bread Champion.

Preheat the oven to 400°F. Sprinkle 1 cup fine cornmeal into 1 pint vigorously boiling water, stirring continuously to prevent lumps. Add ½ tsp. salt and 4 Tbsp. butter. Stir until the butter is melted, and let sit 10 minutes. Beat together vigorously (or blend) 4 medium eggs and 1 cup cold whole milk. Stir the cornmeal mush and the milk-and-egg mix together. Butter a big round or square baking dish or casserole dish, pour in the batter, pop in the oven, reduce the heat to 375°F, and bake until puffed and golden, between 40 minutes and 1 hour. Serve with more butter.

This is the way Lizzie, my grandparents' black cook, born the year the Civil War ended, made it, and taught me to make it, and it is sublime enough to have surpassed scores of other recipes in taste. The Bake Off was at the famous Homestead resort in western Virginia, and judged by their staff.

Hoecakes

This makes a quick and delicious breakfast. Boil 1 pint water with ½ tsp. salt, and sprinkle in slowly some of your home-ground cornmeal—about ⅔ cup, and stir it 1 or 2 minutes until it thickens to the consistency of batter. Meanwhile heat a little bacon grease (or vegetable oil or butter) in a skillet, spoon the mush into the hot fat, and fry like hotcakes, turning once. Serve as they are, or with more butter. Try them with maple syrup. These were described to me by the lady who first made them for me as a child as fare for slaves who often had to cook outdoors. They were supposedly cooked over fires on cleaned and greased hoes—hence the name.

Chess Pie

This is a Virginia favorite using cornmeal as thickener. It probably had an English origin, with the "chess" a misspelling of "cheese," as lemon curd is sometimes called lemon cheese in England. But this method, using cornmeal, is definitely a New World variation.

Make a one-crust piecrust (see recipe on pages 180–81). Preheat oven to 375°F. The filling: Stir together 2 cups white sugar (or 1 cup white and 1 cup brown), and 2 Tbsp. cornmeal. Beat together 4 medium or 3 large eggs, 4 Tbsp. melted butter, 4 Tbsp. milk, 4 Tbsp. lemon juice, and 2 Tbsp. finely grated lemon rind. Stir the dries and the wets together. Modern hint: I peel off the zest of 1 large lemon (or 2 small ones) and put the rind into the food processor with the 2 cups sugar and pulse it until the peel is finely ground. Pour the filling into the shell and bake for 35 to 45 minutes.

During World War II, the women in our town used to make chess pies with vinegar instead of lemon juice, and they were equally tart and wonderful, though not of course specifically lemony. I recall that they used chicken fat sometimes in the crust if there was no lard, and, again, that it tasted just fine. I couldn't wait for Saturdays when I could walk the mile uptown to the garage where the farmer's market was held, and pay a nickel for a chess tart from the farmer's wife who brought them to town to sell.

▧ JERUSALEM ARTICHOKES

The common sunflower, *Helianthus annuus*, has delicious edible seeds, but they are a nuisance to get at. However, the sunflower has many relatives, and among them is a native American plant called *H. tuberosus*, or the "rooted sunflower." (*Helio* is "sun" in Greek, and *anthus* is "flower.") We call this plant the Jerusalem artichoke, though the name is more than misleading. It was discovered by early American explorers who took it to Europe, specifically to Italy, where it was called by the Italian name for sunflowers, *girasole* (meaning "turning toward the sun," which was later corrupted to "Jerusalem"), and to France, where it was dubbed *artichaud de*

Canada, or "Canadian artichoke." The combined name is what we are left with today. The plant is no kin to artichokes, nor is it from Jerusalem.

DESCRIPTION, HABITAT, AND SEASON

This coarse, eight-foot-tall wildflower has broad, rough, serrated alternate leaves on sturdy, hairy, round stems, though at the bottoms of the stems the leaves become opposite. It has in late summer a cheerful yellow daisylike flower about two and a half inches in diameter, with the central disk as well as the petals being yellow. The difficulty in identifying this plant is that many late-summer flowers are similar. Some flowers that look similar have flanges up the main stem, but Jerusalem artichokes have round, rough, and purplish stems, and "fatter" leaves. This is the only plant with yellow-centered yellow flowers that has, when you pull up a main stem, a tuber (or several) at the end. It grows enthusiastically in wastelands, damp woods, roadside ditches, and fields throughout the temperate parts of eastern Canada and the eastern United States.

The flower, which blooms in late summer, identifies the plant for later digging of the tubers. They may be dug after the first frost. The tubers stay fresh underground until they are dug out, so they can be eaten all winter. Freezing does not affect them adversely.

HISTORY AND LORE

Jerusalem artichokes are native to America, and were widely used by the North American Indians. The taste of the tubers is mild, and does resemble artichokes, in that they share a slightly sweetish aftertaste. Truly, they are a treasure for the forager.

To harvest them, dig around the plants anytime after the first frost, and the tubers will appear, the way potatoes do. Scrub them thoroughly to avoid any grit or dirt, and peel parts of them that won't come clean.

R E C I P E S

The irregular 1" to 2" tubers are more like potatoes than anything else, but unlike potatoes, they get tough if overcooked. Once they have been scrubbed clean, and scraped or partially peeled to make certain no dirt remains, they are fine sliced raw into salads, where they add the same kind of crispness as water chestnuts do. They can be lightly sautéed in oil or butter, salted, and served as a vegetable.

Jerusalem Artichoke Salad

Boil the tubers no longer than 10 minutes in salted water, drain, and chop coarsely. Chill. Add a couple of chopped hard-boiled eggs, a small amount of chopped onion, a spoonful of sweet pickle relish, and toss with enough mayonnaise to dress all lightly. Chill and serve on lettuce leaves.

Jerusalem Artichokes au Gratin

Parboil the tubers until they are just beginning to be tender in salted water to which the juice of half a lemon has been added (but be careful not to overcook). Drain, and make a medium white or cream sauce (see recipe on pages 183–84) seasoned with nutmeg, salt, and pepper. Slice or chop the tubers coarsely, mix with enough cream sauce to coat them, and place them in a buttered casserole dish. Sprinkle them with grated cheddar cheese, and broil them only until the cheese bubbles. They should not be overcooked, as they toughen up again with too much cooking. This dish can be served as a vegetable, a luncheon main dish, or a cocktail party dip or spread for crackers.

▨ WILD RICE

Zizania aquatica is a cereal grain, named by Great Lakes Indians, that grows in water; it is misnamed, being no kin to rice. Its name comes from *zizanion*, a wheat field weed. *Aquatica* refers to its growing medium. It is also sometimes called water oats.

Description, Habitat, and Season

Wild rice is the seed of an annual grass, with slender, basally (from the base) branching culms (grass stems) six to ten feet tall. This reedy water grass has light green, long, flat leaves one to two inches across, goldish green seedpods, and a long foxtail cluster at the top. The seeds are long and thin and cylindrical, in papery husks tipped with bristles. The many varieties are naturalized in some places where it grows outside its natural range.

The varieties of wild rice mature in late summer. Euell Gibbons declares that it grows from the Canadian border to the Gulf of Mexico, and is sometimes planted by hunters who want to shoot the birds that the wild rice attracts. However, it is most prevalent around the Great Lakes and throughout southern Canada. It grows along shores, in quiet, shallow waters such as farm ponds and swamps; and it can grow in fresh or brackish water. Some varieties have adapted to the Deep South, though in general wild rice is a cool-climate plant. Its ripe seeds darken a little as they mature.

History and Lore

The Indians who lived around the Great Lakes made constant use of the grain. Their method of harvesting has never been improved upon: Among the mature reeds, pull a handful down over your boat, and whack them sharply with a stick. The grains should then dislodge into your boat. (If they don't, try again in several days.) You can put a sheet in the bottom of the boat to catch the grains and gather them up more easily. Peterson warns of ergot, which is a deadly fungus that sometimes replaces the grains in corn, rye, wild rice, and other grains. The ergot grains will be a different color from the other tan, brown, or blackish grains, usually purple but sometimes pink or reddish. If they are present, either pick them out carefully or do not use the rice. They will be similar to the rice in shape, but often larger.

R E C I P E S

Once home, the grain must be dried for several days, parched in the sun for a day, or parched in the oven by putting the grains in shallow pans at 275°F for about 1 hour, stirring often so they parch evenly.

Finally, the rice must be husked by rubbing the cooled grains between the palms. It can then be stored in a glass jar, tightly sealed, or in a glass jar or plastic bag in the freezer.

Boiled Wild Rice

When you are ready to use the rice, wash it thoroughly in three bowls of cold water, skimming off any husks that rise to the top. Do this until no more husks rise, then cook it as you would rice, in this case 1 measure grain to 3 measures water, salted, boiled for over ½ hour, or until the water is absorbed. You can also cook it in seasoned broth. I add a bay leaf, and sometimes a packet of dried onion soup. It is especially good with game of any kind, but I like it with morels (see chapter 3).

Popped Rice

I have fried dry rice and wild rice by heating peanut oil to about 375°F, and as it heats, dropping in a grain at a time, until it suddenly puffs up in the hot oil. That tells you the temperature is right. Then you slowly add 1 to 2 Tbsp. dry wild rice, or dry white rice, or some combination. Almost at once, the grains pop and swell to double their size, and are wonderful scattered on top of soup or salad, or just salted and eaten as you would popcorn.

Oriental Salad

Gather a bunch of spring greens (see chapter 2), wash and dry them, and toss them with popped rice and the following dressing.

Oriental Salad Dressing

This dressing may make enough to use for several salads. Mix in a jar with a tight lid 4 chopped cloves garlic, 1 knob fresh ginger the size of your thumb, grated, 2 Tbsp. dark sesame oil (available in grocery stores among Asian food products), 1/2 cup peanut oil, 1/4 cup orange or tangerine juice, 2 Tbsp. lemon juice, and 2 Tbsp. soy sauce. This dressing has a distinctive and different flavor. Shake well before dressing the greens lightly with it. The leftover dressing will last in the refrigerator at least a couple of weeks.

▣ HORSERADISH

While you're gathering spring greens, you can dig your year's supply of horserad-ish, to be grated with vinegar and cream. Horseradish (*Armoracia lapathifolia,* dock-leafed horseradish, or *A. rusti-cana,* rustic horseradish) came with the English settlers, and escaped into the wild. The name suggests that it was first identified in Armorica, an ancient name for northwest

Gaul. *Lapathifolia* is likely from the Latin *labi*, "to fall," kin to our words *lapse*, a falling away, and *lap*, to fold over (*folia* is "leaves"), for the leaves have the appearance of falling away from the plant, and have slightly wavy edges.

DESCRIPTION, HABITAT, AND SEASON

Horseradish is a perennial with a long, white, irregular root. Its dark, tough, wavy, scalloped, heavily veined leaves about a foot long and two to six inches across spring from a channeled stalk out from the root. Horseradish has tiny white flowers in early summer (May to July) that grow higher than the leaves, and out of a central stalk. It grows in fields, pastures, roadsides, and especially along river-banks and creeksides. As it will grow a new plant from only the tiniest portion of a root left in the ground, it is sometimes found in fairly thick clumps. Spring to fall is the time to gather it by digging up the fat, long root.

HISTORY AND LORE

Horseradish, with its pungency, has a long history as a medical stim-ulant. Many Indian tribes employed it to stimulate glandular activity, to combat scurvy, and as a diaphoretic (perspiration-inducing) "loos-ening" treatment for the common cold. It is believed to aid digestion of rich, fatty foods; thus it is most often paired culinarily with roast meats. Euell Gibbons warns about cooking it, for heat destroys the flavor and quality.

RECIPES

Horseradish doesn't release its pungent smell until it's grated. One root is probably all you need for a year's supply. In addition, the young leaves of the plant are pungent, but make a good potherb when mixed with some milder greens.

Prepared Horseradish

Grate scrubbed, cleaned horseradish root finely into a bowl of salted water, or shred it in the food processor and pour it from there into salted water. Drain it well, and pack the horseradish in a jar. Cover it with white vinegar and store it in the refrigerator. To serve, add it to tomato catsup or salsa to taste for cocktail sauce, or best of all, fold it into salted whipped cream or commercial sour cream to accompany beef or venison.

▣ SASSAFRAS

Sassafras is a flavor nearly everyone loves; sassafras root is what root beer was originally made of. *Sassafras albidum,* sometimes called *S. officinale,* grows abundantly everywhere in the East, from Canada to Florida. It was first discovered by early French settlers in Florida, and the name is of unknown origin, though possibly the French had it from a local Indian name for the plant.

DESCRIPTION, HABITAT, AND SEASON

Sassafras is generally a small tree, though it may grow to a hundred feet tall. It is readily identified in thickets and woods and wood marges by its four leaf patterns, a left and right mitten, a simple (plain) leaf, and a three-lobed leaf. The leaves are bright green, smooth, smooth edged, and fragrant. The twigs, or new branchlets, are pale green. In the spring it has clusters of fragrant yellow flowers. The entire plant, but especially the root, smells like root beer.

HISTORY AND LORE

Sassafras has figured in folklore ever since the English colonized North America, and was known by the English before they got here. A shipload of sassafras root leaving Virginia for London in 1609 was North America's first export. The plant had already, in the century of Spanish exploration of the Western Hemisphere, gained a nearly magical reputation. Called ague tree and tea tree, sassafras was reputed to cure many ailments, from broken bones to fevers, from worms to baldness. Modern herbals classify sassafras as a weak antiseptic. The root bark was believed to be the most potent part of the plant.

Today we know that it should be used with caution, if at all, for the entire plant (part of the laurel family, which contains many poisonous plants) contains a compound, safrole, that is mildly carcinogenic. Yet my grandmother believed this tea "thinned your blood" in springtime in preparation for the coming hot weather, so I drank the pinkish tea with her every spring from 1943 on—and often at other times of the year. The leaves we collected, dried, and crumbled into the fragrant powder called filé by the Cajuns were used to thicken the gumbos that my grandmother's cook occasionally made.

Unfortunately, today, because of its carcinogenic nature, the root cannot legally be bought or sold; yet the flavor, now artificially made, remains popular in soft drinks, medicines, soaps, and toothpastes.

RECIPES

Sassafras Tea

Dig sassafras roots in late winter or early spring, clean them well, chop them up a bit, and boil a handful in 1 quart water for about 10 or 20 minutes.

Filé

Filé is the spring leaves of sassafras dried and pulverized. It is a thickening, seasoning agent added (1 Tbsp. for a regular recipe) at the end of the cooking time, just before serving, and lends a smooth, slippery quality to gumbo and other Creole dishes.

▣ GINSENG

Ginseng, *Panax quinquefolius,* is the most interesting plant I know. Its scientific name, from the Greek words *pan* ("all") and *akos* ("cure") is closely kin to the word *panacea,* meaning "cure-all." The word *ginseng* comes from the Chinese *jin-chen,* a word meaning "man-root"; and *quinquefolius* refers to the usual five-leaf arrangement of each prong emerging from the main stem of the foot-high plant.

Although ginseng is not exactly edible, it is mysterious and very exotic, and I believe it deserves inclusion among the best of wild foods. In 1995, good Appalachian ginseng root properly dried brought its diggers $430 a pound. In specialty stores it is enormously expensive, sometimes bringing up to ten thousand dollars an *ounce.* The most lucrative markets for the plant are in the Far East. The mystery is, and always has been: Why?

DESCRIPTION, HABITAT, AND SEASON

Ginseng is a common name for several of the plants in the family, including Chinese, American, and Korean ginsengs. The family otherwise includes English ivy, the rice-paper plant of China, and sarsaparilla. This small and unprepossessing plant has a series of long, slender stems, sometimes dark red in color, each with five leaves emerging from the top, a tiny, insignificant whitish or reddish flower in the spring, and come fall, a bright red berry cluster in the middle, from which come the seeds that will eventually, if the plant is left alone, fall and take root in the soil nearby. First-year plants have only three leaves to a branch, and the berries are lighter red, sometimes yellowish. Only in the third year do the plants develop the characteristic five leaves.

Neither seeds nor leaves have any uses. Ginseng's value is all underground. As the plant dies back each year, and puts out a new stalk each spring, there remain at the top of the root right at ground level the scars from the previous year's stalks. These bumps or wrinkles at the top of the root, called the coils, where the stem emerges from the ground, can be "read" for age like the rattles of a rattlesnake or the rings on a tree trunk.

Ginseng is undeniably hard to find. As much time as I spend in the woods, I have not seen more than a dozen plants in my life, all of them young. Obstacles, dangerous and tiring, do not daunt the hunters. The harder the going gets, the more the diggers' efforts will meet with success; the more isolated and unattainable the area, the more likely it is (they believe) that they will find the plant. There seems to reside in lifelong hunters the belief that only the virtuous among them can find the plant, and that the dangers only exist to frighten away cowards and weaklings.

HISTORY AND LORE

The plants are steeped in lore. Ginseng was an article of tribute (demanded by the emperor) as early as the T'ang dynasty in China, which began in 618 A.D.

This small and ordinary-looking shrub was first recorded in China about four thousand years ago. It grows in the mountains in only the Northern Hemisphere of our planet. The states where it is found most commonly are Virginia and West Virginia, Pennsylvania, North Carolina, Tennessee, and Georgia. These days, however, it is so overpicked as to be rare every place it grows, from Canada to Florida, and from Quebec west to Manitoba. Ginseng is now *cultivated* in the Great Lakes states, primarily in Wisconsin and Michigan.

Panax ginseng, the oriental variety that grows in Korea and northern China, is believed to have many palliative medicinal qualities; but *Panax quinquefolius*, the American variety, is even more valued by Asians. Perversely, Americans overwhelmingly prefer Asian ginseng.

Today, some say ginseng glows in the dark and that it moves around—literally uprooting and changing location. It is reputed to shriek if yanked rudely out of the soil. It is said to grow only in tandem with certain other trees—mainly a variety of hardwoods (but no agreement can be had on which ones)—and never in fields, valleys, marshes, river bottoms, or exposed places. One hunter told me that it will not grow for three years on land devastated by a forest fire. Another told me it grew on the shady sides of deep gullies in the mountains. But some believe it grows only on a mountain's cool and duffy north slope. 'Sang diggers say that the plant occurs only by itself, not gregariously (though in the virgin forests in the early days of European occupation, it reportedly grew in huge colonies and sometimes spread across many acres). It supposedly won't grow anywhere near metal. It is rumored—perhaps to discourage competition—to share its habitat intimately with copperheads and rattlers.

I hold in my hand a fresh root. Sniffing it closely, I smell nothing but earth, dirt. I bite off a piece, and chew. The first impression is bitter, peculiar, and then a mild sweetness and a flavor fleetingly like—maybe ginger?—comes through. Although I chew and chew, the root does not diminish in my mouth. I wait after I've spit it out, wondering if it really banishes hunger and thirst, as it's reputed to do.

What is it that makes this plant so valuable? It seems that the primary reason for such astonishing prices for a wild plant is that ginseng root is, as most folks know, widely believed to be an aphrodisiac. In China today, when an elderly relative begins to feel the effects of age upon his sex drive or just in general, a family may go into debt to buy ginseng, sometimes enough for only one dose. Of course, if one's general health gets a boost, it follows that one's sexual vitality may also be reawakened.

Ginseng, whatever clinical trials show, or do not show, apparently works often enough to keep up the trade. One Chinese physician told me that Chinese ginseng is a "hot" medicine, and that the American disposition, being already hot and overstimulated, would perhaps not profit so much from Chinese ginseng as would the cooler Asian nature. American ginseng, he said, is the essence of yin, or feminine energy, and is therefore ideally suited for American consumption.

Have you ever known anyone who was cured by ginseng of a really serious illness? I ask, over and over again. The answers are never definitive.

Asians chew the root, brew tea from the root, and scrape the dried root into hot water to make a drink. Ginseng is part of a high percentage of Asian herbal remedies, which include some truly alarming ingredients like poisonous sea plants, jellyfish, insects, and various kinds of dried lizards and toads. There are as many opinions about dosage and frequency of use as there are users.

Native Americans, notably the Chippewa, treated various illnesses, including heart trouble, with ginseng. Probably the Doctrine of Signatures is at work here, which, as mentioned earlier, states that any plant's uses to man are suggested by its shape or color. Ginseng, according to this thinking, is believed to have many properties mysteriously relating to man because its shape, occasionally a trunk and four limbs and, rarely, a small rootlet where a penis ought to be, suggests the shape of man.

Some medical studies have concluded that the well-known placebo effect matches the effect of most medicines; it is common in double-blind drug tests to have a high percentage of the placebo users respond to the drug they *think* they are taking.

Yet pharmaceutical companies have tried in vain to discover what it is that ginseng contains. Controlled studies, literally hundreds of them, have yielded contradictory results. Korean tests report that ginseng "facilitated mating behavior" in rats. Tests in this country remain inconclusive. In Russia, scientists have continually tested ginseng's results. In one study among Russian factory workers, volunteers who took a mere four milligrams of ginseng a day lost significantly fewer days at work due to colds, sinus, bronchial, and tonsil infections, and influenza than their fellow workers who did not take ginseng.

Other studies have indicated that Siberian ginseng users proved able to endure noise, stress, extremes of hot and cold, and long hours of hard labor much more readily than nonusers.

Other tests indicate that people hospitalized with problems such as insomnia, neurosis, or anxiety responded more frequently and profoundly to Siberian ginseng than to other drugs.

Eastern and Western medicine may not be as far apart as they once were. For the brisk business and high price of ginseng in America are evidence that we are just as willing as the Chinese to believe in its general efficacy. And maybe there is something to ginseng, particularly if, in addition to using it, we guard our health by not smoking, by eating and drinking moderately, and by taking regular exercise!

R E C I P E S

Ginseng Tea

Shave off 1 tsp. or so ginseng root, fresh or dried, and steep it for 3 to 10 minutes in a small pot of boiling water. Then drink it. How often? Three times a day. Once a day. Every day for a week.

Ginseng Cordial

Into 1 gallon of excellent bourbon or brandy, place 1 large ginseng root at least 5" long. Close the bottle and let it sit for 3 months before drinking 1 oz. a day. This is said to be a sure palliative for rheumatism and arthritis. When the whiskey is gone, the root can be used the same way at least two more times.

◼ MAPLE SYRUP

Acer saccharum is the sugar maple. Its name is kin to our acre and agriculture, and *saccharum* means "sweet."

DESCRIPTION, HABITAT, AND SEASON

We have over 150 species of maple trees in the North Temperate Zones. Many of them are planted along streets as shade trees, or along country lanes or roads. Most of them have leaves that turn brilliant reds, oranges, and yellows in autumn. The leaves are generally opposite and simple, with 3 or 5 lobes. It takes some expertise to tell one from another. But all of them have sap that rises in early spring, when the nights are below freezing and the days above. Among these is *Acer saccharum,* the sugar maple. That one is supposed to be the best, but you couldn't prove it by me. I've tried syrup from many, and they all taste about the same, including syrup from the box elder, which is the only maple with compound leaves. Maples are so common in our cities and countryside that you needn't go far to find one.

The forest service says the tapping won't hurt the trees if it is done right, and proof of that is the maple syrup industry in New England, which taps the same trees year after year for the sap. It is easy to tap the tree for the watery sap that, boiled down, makes maple syrup and maple sugar. Even if all you get from your own attempt at sugaring is a cup of the lovely dark syrup, do it once so you'll know how, and then you'll probably want to do it again, year after year.

Just a wet stain on the side of a maple tree on a sunny February afternoon may be your signal. Look for sap dripping from a cut branch, and you'll know the time is right.

When it first comes from the tree the sap is so diluted that you can't taste any sweetness at all. So to obtain syrup, you must boil it down to about one-fourtieth of its original amount. That's about forty gallons of sap to make one gallon of maple syrup. It sounds daunting, but your buckets or cans fill rapidly, and the water boils away rapidly, especially if you start the syrup out of doors.

All you need do is drill a hole with a half-inch drill, about two inches into a maple tree, three to six feet above ground, aimed *slightly upward* into the tree. When you hit the layer where the sap is, the tree will immediately begin to drip. So go slowly, and stop when you hit the sap layer.

Then you insert a spile, an inexpensive, graduated metal spout with a hook on top to hold a bucket, to channel the sap out of the tree and into your container. You can also use half-inch plastic tubing, which can lead to a container sitting on the ground; a fat plastic straw; or a small metal pipe. For the truly intrepid, a half-inch hollow tube can be made from an elderberry stem with the center pulp bored out. A very large, very old tree may sustain as many as four or even more taps, on different sides and at slightly different heights. The size of the tree should be your guide. (We have one wonderful old maple that measures sixteen feet around, and I put four taps into it most years.) Open wounds and sawed-off branches will yield sap, so a container may be placed to catch that, too.

R E C I P E S

Strain or filter the collected sap into a pan with a large open surface, such as a flat baking pan. We do the first boiling outdoors, where the fire smells sweet and the wind drives off the water vapor more quickly, but you can do this in your kitchen, too.

Then you simply boil the sap down, adding more as your sap containers fill. You don't stir it, but you can skim off the foam as it forms. Keep the pan simmering. Obviously, it is getting denser all the time. As it boils down and begins to form a blanket of tiny bubbles, it is nearly done. If you are working outside, remove the pan from the fire, and finish it on a stove indoors where you can watch it carefully, and adjust the heat to keep the syrup from scorching. You will know when it's ready by the profusion of tiny little bubbles all over, as well as from the color and taste of pure maple syrup. I always pour it through a fine sieve at the end, just in case any bark or soot has fallen in while it cooked.

Maple Sugar Cubes or Leaves

(This is not my favorite way to use maple syrup. The blocks it makes are hard and dense, albeit pure, and don't melt in the mouth the way the following recipe, for Maple Fondant, does. If you want to make pure maple sugar, though, follow these directions carefully.)

To turn maple syrup into sugar, start with 2 to 3 cups cooled, strained syrup. The amount doesn't particularly matter, as you don't add anything else. Heat it with a candy thermometer in an open pan slowly, without stirring, until it reaches hard-thread consistency, 233°F. Check by both methods, candy thermometer (which may vary with altitude) *and* the cold-water test (test by dropping a few drops into a cup of cold water, then reaching in with a fork and tugging at the syrup. Does it pull out into a thread? If not, it isn't ready.) When it makes a stiff thread and has reached 233°F, take it off the heat and leave it alone with the thermometer still in it until it has cooled to 110°F. At that point, add a little vanilla, about 1 tsp.,

I recently discovered an easier way to test candy than the cold-water method, my own "cold-plate" method. Place three or four little saucers in the freezer before you start your candy. Instead of having to fish around in ice water for the ball of candy, drop a few drops onto one of the cold plates fresh out of the freezer, then see if it forms a soft ball, or a hard thread, or whatever.

and beat it until it turns a pale color and is stiff enough to hold a shape. I use a handheld electric beater, but you can use a wooden spoon. Pour or scrape it into a buttered square pan, or press the sugar into maple leaf molds sprayed lightly with vegetable spray, and put it into airtight containers. I like it with the vanilla, but if you are a purist, you can leave that out.

Sublime Maple Fondant
(Follow this exactly for best results.)

Stir together over low heat 1 cup maple syrup, 2 cups sugar, ¾ cup half and half, 2 Tbsp. butter, and ¼ tsp. cream of tartar. Cook until they come to a gentle boil. Put a candy thermometer into the pot, and cook this mixture slowly and without stirring or disturbing until it reaches the soft-ball stage, or 238°F. This may take about 45 minutes.

Test it with the thermometer and with the cup of cold water. When it has reached about 238°F and when a drop of the syrup makes a nice flat, soft ball on the bottom of a cup of cold water, slide it off the heat, leave the thermometer in it, and let it cool undisturbed to 110°F. This may take 1 hour or so. Add a little vanilla, and beat until it turns creamy—or pull it with buttered hands into silvery taffy.

Cut or shape this into individual candies, and in a short time it will transform itself into smooth, creamy fondant, possibly the best melt-in-your mouth candy in the world.

Maple Nut Meringue Goodies
(Makes one dozen delightful light, chewy confections.)

Heat oven to 275°F or 280°F. Beat 2 egg whites with a pinch of salt and a pinch of cream of tartar until stiff. Gradually beat in ⅓ cup maple syrup, stir in ⅛ to ⅓ cup wild nut meats, and drop by Tbsp. onto a vegetable oil–sprayed cookie sheet. Slow-bake until browned, possibly as long as 1 hour, then let cool in the oven. Store in an airtight container or eat at once.

Maple Custard

Preheat oven to 350°F. Beat or blend together 4 eggs, ¾ cup maple syrup, 1 tsp. vanilla, a few grains salt—and 2 cups of either milk or half and half, or even heavy cream. (I use some combination of the above.) Pour into a soufflé dish, and bake in a larger pan of hot water until the middle is set. Note: In custard, the more yolks, the more tender and creamy the custard will be, and the more whites, the firmer. Of course, the more yolks, the richer in calories and cholesterol. So, using the basic ingredients here, try omitting the whites, which will give you a creamier custard; or doubling the number of yolks, which will give you a richer custard; or cutting down to 2 yolks and using 4 whites, to reduce calories.

Any way you make it, it's a delicious dessert, or a gift that will tempt an invalid to eat.

▦ AVOCADOS

A native of the West Indies, the avocado (*Persea americana*) is a member of the laurel family. The name is from an Aztec word, *ahuacatl*. The Latin name, intended to convey exoticism, suggests wrongly that the fruit is an "American Persian." The folk name, alligator pear, comes about because of the scaliness of the rind, though it might possibly indicate a propinquity between the fruit and the animal.

In the continental United States there are technically no wild avocados; yet Floridians tell me that some trees have escaped from cultivation to grow wild wherever it is warm enough. Some varieties grow in California, and others in Florida, but frosts farther north regularly kill them.

DESCRIPTION, HABITAT, AND SEASON

Though we nearly always treat it as a vegetable, the avocado is in fact a fruit. The tree upon which it grows is fairly small, about the size of an apple tree, or no taller than about twenty feet. The leaves are large, oblong, with prominent veins, and the fruit pulp is about the size and shape of a pear, but dark green with a leathery rind. From the outside it looks the same green or ripe. When it's ready to eat, it falls to the ground. But when you buy one in the supermarket, it is ripe when it loses its rock hardness and yields just a little to the touch. Then the mellow nutty fruit will be creamy, mild, and yellow or yellow-green, surrounding a large round seed. All it needs is salt and pepper and a drop or two of lemon juice for a wonderful snack, for lunch, or tossed in a salad. In some parts of South America, avocados are treated as fruit: that is, they are sugared and served with whipped cream or ice cream, or in a mélange with other fruits.

Once when I was in Florida in late November to swim with dolphins, the motel where I stayed backed up to what seemed to be a wild avocado grove in full ripeness. When I asked the motel owner about whose it was, and whether I might poach, he hitched up his tattered bermudas and shrugged. It was like being in King Croesus' garden to be able to go across the little sandy path and pick up a ripe avocado off the ground whenever I wanted. I was told that animals eat them in the wild, but this was right along Highway 1, and there were few wild animals about.

R E C I P E S

Guacamole

Cut the flesh out of 2 avocados. Sprinkle with the strained juice of 1 lemon. Add a light sprinkle of salt and some chili powder (start with 1 tsp., and add until you get the taste right), and add 2 to 4 crushed cloves of garlic. Add black or red pepper if you want. Mix well with a fork, and serve with corn tortillas, cut into quarters and fried quickly in hot vegetable oil. This makes a wonderful light lunch.

Cream of Avocado Soup

Cut 1 avocado's meat into little cubes, sprinkle with lemon juice, and set aside. Mash 2 or 3 ripe avocados (seeded and peeled) with 1 Tbsp. Worcestershire sauce, a little lemon juice, and a little minced fresh onion (and a small crushed garlic clove if you like) in a bowl. Add to it 2 cups good chicken broth, and mix well. If you want it perfectly smooth, blend it or force it through a ricer at this point, but I don't. Transfer to a saucepan, and heat it slowly to not quite boiling, and add 1 cup whipping cream. Mix well, cover, and bring to a near-boil again. Taste, correct seasoning, and serve immediately, with the cubes on top for garnish. Makes over 1 quart.

▣ PRICKLY PEAR

Throughout not only the desert regions of this country, but also dry fields nearly everywhere, can be found four or five similar species of the native American genus *Opuntia*. Prickly pear, also called Indian fig and tuna, is easily recognized by its flat, round pads (stems, really). It is well protected by dangerous spines and by its pear-shaped spiny fruits, which develop from the yellow flowers and are green at first, then either yellow, dark red, or reddish purple.

Both pads and fruit are not only edible but delicious, though both must be gathered carefully with leather gloves or by burning or cutting off the spines before picking. The fruit may ripen at any time throughout the summer and fall, and the pads are good to eat whenever you find them.

RECIPES

Prickly Pear Pads

Handle carefully! Rid the pads of spines by cutting them off, burning them off, or knocking them off. Then rinse the pads, slice into string bean–size lengths, and use as you would a string bean, cooking them about the same length of time. They may be chilled and added to salads. I had a wonderful dish in Mexico once that I have replicated satisfactorily: Cubes of lean pork are stir-fried in olive oil with sliced onion, minced garlic, chili powder, and sliced prickly pear pads. When done, season to taste and serve on rice. The pads add an okra-like mucilaginous quality that is smooth and pleasant.

Prickly Pear Jam

The fruit of prickly pear can be eaten as is, like any other fresh fruit, but it also makes a lovely red jam. It is not very tart, so it needs lemon juice. After removing the spines of ripe fruit, chop or pulverize the fruit, add 2 Tbsp. lemon juice to 1 cup fruit, and add an equal amount of sugar. Cook slowly until thickened, stirring frequently.

▦ WATERMELON RIND

Citrullus vulgaris is the Latin name for watermelons. They do not grow wild in America (though many members of the family, such as crookneck squash and pumpkin, do), so if I were to describe where to forage them, I'd be advocating stealing. Instead, I'm advocating a different kind of foraging, the kind that can be done at picnics and church suppers. All you have to do is to surreptitiously (or obviously) gather up the leftover rinds of the watermelon, *Citrullus vulgaris,* or the "citruslike gourd," after folks are finished devouring their pink slices. Any variety will do. Put them in a plastic bag and take them home. The only other way to make watermelon rind pickles is to actually go out and buy a watermelon, and eat it yourself, saving the rind. These pickles are definitely the best in the world, and in my growing-up years there were few midday dinners that didn't have watermelon rind pickles to accompany whatever else there was: chicken, beef, lamb, venison. Jars of these make great presents, and everyone loves them!

R E C I P E S

Watermelon Rind Pickles
(This process requires five days.)

Day 1: Take the rind of 1 large watermelon, wash it in several waters, and trim off the hard green rind and the soft, crisp red fruit, keeping only the white. Cut the rind into 1" squares (smaller is also fine). Put the cubes in a large bowl or a small plastic or enamel dishpan, add 1 cup pickling lime (available in the canning section of groceries), fill it to the top of the rind with water, and stir it well. Weigh it down to keep the rind submerged, and keep it in the lime for 24 hours.

Because the lime settles more or less at once, you must stir it up and turn the pieces every time you think of it, to redistribute the lime in the water, and move the rind around.

Day 2: After a day, feel a piece of the rind for crispness. Wash the rind in several waters until the water is clear, to wash away the excess lime.

Make a syrup of 5 lbs. sugar, 3 pints cider vinegar, and a handful of each of the following whole spices: cloves, ginger, allspice, celery seed, cracked nutmeg or mace, and cinnamon sticks. Boil the mixture and stir until the sugar is dissolved. Pour the fruit into the boiling syrup, cut the heat off, and let it stand (covered) for 24 more hours.

Day 3: Bring the pickles in the syrup to a boil. At once, give them a stir, cut the heat off, and then let them sit for another day.

Day 4: Repeat day 3.

Day 5: Bring the pickles in syrup to a boil, and boil them for 1 hour. Pick out the rind squares, and pack them up in sterilized jars. Strain the syrup, and fill each jar of pickles to the top. Wipe the edges and screw down the clean lids carefully. No sealing is necessary if the jars and lids are clean and the pickles are used within the year. My grandmother called these Seven-Day Pickles, and stretched the process out by adding two more boils. But 5 days is plenty.

Finally, this method will work beautifully with any number of vegetables and fruits. I've used zucchini, overlarge cucumbers, yellow squash, and other melon rinds through the years. Once there was a frost warning when we still had unripe tomatoes on the vines, so I made green tomato pickles using this method. I've never failed to get good pickles.

ANUAL FORAGERS' CALENDAR

Human beings like clear boundaries. Nature is continuous, but we want divisions. Thus this calendar, less calendar really than reminder, so that you won't forget to go looking for something wild that you really intended to look for. Calendars of things that grow must necessarily be vague, for they are subject not only to specific latitudes but also to early or late frosts, much or little rain, mountainous or flat locales, hot or cold seasons, and other variables. An example is that this year, because of record late frosts that nipped them in the bud, we got no crab apples. And because our spring this year was very late as well as wetter than usual, the morels were later than usual. So this is a general and approximate friendly reminder.

In the late winter, rest and dream, take a month off. As bears know, everyone needs to hibernate for a while.

Early spring. When the nights are still frozen, but the days bring thaws, begin checking maples for sap to gather and boil.

When the ground is thawed, and green things begin to appear, look for dandelion greens. Begin your search for fiddleheads. Collect sassafras root in the woods.

Soon after, when the ground is unlikely to frost again, a million spring greens appear. Begin to look for lambs'-quarters, watercress, poke, and sorrel now. Morels start growing, and fruit for at least a month, especially if the winter has saturated the ground.

Among the first things to bloom is elderberry, with its flat white bounty. On the ground you will find violets to candy.

As the green plants leap into light, begin to look for wild asparagus, chicory, ramps.

When there are no more morels, when the days begin to feel like summer but the nights are still cold, in that between-spring-and-summer time, begin to look for wild strawberries. Lambs'-quarters ought to be prolific by now. Look for milkweed and nettles. Sorrel will continue to grow all summer. This is the prime of the watercress harvest. Look for spring coprinus mushrooms. Dig horseradish. This is the time of year that rewards foragers most richly.

As summer begins, if it rains, look for puffballs. Now, while they are still as small as Ping-Pong balls, pick walnuts for pickling. Lambs'-quarters are thriving.

As the sun reaches its northernmost point, black raspberries begin. Gather June apples. Make mint jelly, and keep some mint to dry for tea. Pick catnip for drying. Add nasturtiums to salads.

In midsummer, pickle the brined walnuts. Wineberries fruit in the mid-Atlantic states, raspberries elsewhere. Begin looking in wet woods for chanterelles and sulfur shelf mushrooms. Some crab apples ripen. At a July 4th party, collect up watermelon rinds at a picnic and make pickles. Two or three weeks after, wineberries and raspberries (black and red), and blackberries begin to be ripe. Candy some roses.

In late summer, look for blueberries and huckleberries. Land cress is wonderful from now into cold weather. Figs ripen. After rain, look for puffballs and field mushrooms. In the woods, search for boletes. Coprini are likely to be around again. Oyster mushrooms begin growing about now. Elderberries ripen. Wild rice is ready to harvest. This is the time to make jellies and pickles. Some apples ripen now.

In very late summer, plums and cherries ripen. From now on, field mushrooms and puffballs will fruit overnight in warm, wet weather. Land cress is bursting.

As summer turns to fall, look for wild cherries. Apples. Pears ripen. As the days grow longer, grapes ripen. So do figs.

When the weather begins to turn chilly at night, pecans fall. Ginseng season begins, continuing to frost. After frost, dig the first Jerusalem artichokes. This is the time for boletes.

In the late fall, after some frosty nights, gather black walnuts, hickories, beechnuts. Pick wild mustard. Gather fall apples and have a cider party. Look for rose hips. Collect abandoned ears of corn. Quinces ripen and can be made into marmalade.

In early winter, begin to look for cranberries. Take a trip to Florida and gather some coconuts and avocados. You can still gather wild mustard. Now is the time to draw a chair close to the fire and pick nuts. And in December, give as gifts marmalade or apple butter, dried mint, flavored vinegars, maple syrup, catnip mice, a ginseng root in a bottle of whiskey, some pickled watermelon rind or fruit jelly redolent of summer. Buy yourself a new pair of comfy walking shoes for Christmas!

THE
LAST WORD

An interest in wild foods is a healthy hobby, and it's a hobby that gets us out and going, that makes us move. And of course there's some brain exercising going on as we attempt to distinguish between one hickory and another, or to remember a location, or keep separate the identifications of many plants. Knowing the outside world around us reestablishes the links we have broken with nature and the seasons. I take seriously the idea of hunting and eating wild foods. It's what we all started out doing, eons ago. Cultivating an interest in gathering and cooking at the very least means more respect for the world that sustains us as well as healthier diets.

After all, there may be a real health benefit in using wild foods in our diets. Despite miraculous medical advances, the evidence is that we are not very well nourished in our modern civilizations. We know some of the reasons, of course: smoking, too much fat, too little exercise. But optimum health continues to evade us.

Everything we eat that is grown commercially is grown in depleted soils or soils artificially and often only periodically fertilized. Of course there are some nutrients in such foods, but a food can only be as good as the soil in which it is grown. Only wild foods found in pastures, woodlands, on the edges of streams and rivers, in wild places, are grown in something akin to real, mineral-rich soil that has not been tampered with. Perhaps the tiny amounts of trace minerals in such foods can make a real difference in our health. In fact, a physician friend of mine has suggested that perhaps it is the tiny traces of minerals we never ordinarily ingest that makes wild ginseng the healer it is reputed to be.

Sharing wild foods is one of life's joys. I love serving morels to guests, and listening to them rave, or having for a dinner party a salad I have gathered of wild greens, dark and tasty, perhaps dotted with violet blossoms. Wild foods make wonderful presents and great hostess gifts. It means a lot to have someone drop off a bunch of fresh asparagus, bound in cheery ribbon, in May, or bring by a jar of homemade apple butter as thanks for having been included in a party. A basket of several kinds of jelly makes a lovely birthday gift. You'll find your own ways to share your bounty.

One wonderful old mountain man whom I interviewed several years ago on the subject of folk medicine said to me, "If it works, it's good. If it don't, it's worthless. Sometimes you can't tell if it's the medicine or the person's own body that done the healing. But that's true of that fancy medicine with doctors and hospitals, now ain't it?" Either nature heals the body, or the body heals itself. Foraging is a wonderful inexpensive path to wellness.

I wish for everyone who has this book in hand happy foraging, delicious cooking, and vibrant good health!

APPENDIX
BASIC RECIPES

Beef Broth

(This is a substitute for canned consommé
or beef broth or bouillon. It's cheaper,
very good, and you can control the salt.)

Brown in a 350°F oven 2 lbs. marrow bones, those rings of bone
with the soft interiors sometimes labeled "soup bones." Ask your
butcher if none are on display. When they begin to sizzle, add a
couple of onions, stir them into the fat that the meat has already ren-
dered, return to the oven, and keep browning until the bones are dark.
Remove from the oven, place in a large kettle, add ½ tsp. peppercorns, 6 cloves, 2 bay leaves, 2 carrots, 2 stalks celery (and some
leaves), some parsley and thyme if you wish, and 1 gallon water. *No
salt.* Bring this to a boil, reduce the heat, and cook slowly for 2 to 3
hours, or until it's reduced to about half. Strain it, cool it, refrigerate
it. When the fat is solid, remove it all. Then freeze the broth in small
portions for easy future use. Add salt when you thaw and use it.

Chicken Broth

Do everything the same way, only use leftover chicken parts, such as necks, backs, gizzards, or hearts, and 1 Tbsp. oil.

Vegetable Broth

If you are a vegetarian, melt a little butter (or use oil), and stir into it several coarsely chopped stalks celery, 6 cloves, 2 bay leaves, 1 sprig thyme, 2 crushed garlic cloves, 1 turnip (optional), 1 chopped pepper (optional), and 1 big chopped onion. Bake the vegetables uncovered in the oven for $\frac{1}{2}$ hour. Boil 6 cups water, add the veggies, and keep boiling. Reduce it by boiling to about 1 quart, and that, strained, is your broth.

Mayonnaise

In a food processor or blender, put the following: 2 Tbsp. fresh lemon juice or 2 Tbsp. cider vinegar, 1 egg, 1 tsp. salt, 1 clove garlic, peeled, 1 tsp. Dijon mustard. Measure 1 cup safflower, peanut, or corn oil, or olive oil. Turn the food processor on high. After 15 seconds, *slowly* pour in the cup of oil, over the course of 1 minute. The final product will look like store-bought mayonnaise, but taste better. Keep it in the refrigerator, and use it within 2 weeks. Mayonnaise makes better on a clear than on a rainy day.

Salad Dressing
(Makes 1 cup or so.)

Mix $\frac{3}{4}$ cup olive oil with $\frac{1}{4}$ cup good vinegar (cider, wine, flavored, balsamic, etc.), and 2 Tbsp. fresh lemon juice. Add 1 or 2 cloves crushed garlic, $\frac{1}{2}$ tsp. salt, $\frac{1}{2}$ tsp. coarse ground pepper, and $\frac{1}{2}$ tsp. sugar. That's what gives the palate joy: zing, salt, piquancy. Shake it up well. That's the basic mix, and is just fine by itself. I make it in a pint jar with a tight-fitting screw-on lid. It keeps in the fridge for as long as a month. I use sparing amounts on salads and cold vegetables.

For variety, add anything else you fancy, such as 1 tsp. dry or prepared mustard, honey or more sugar, some herbs or capers, or both, a dash of Worcestershire sauce, soy sauce, paprika, or tomato paste, 1 tsp. poppy seeds, 1" to 2" anchovy paste, or any combination of the above.

Soufflé

Soufflés are elegant, and very versatile. I made my first for some boy when I was fifteen. It was a colossal failure. To make it worse, the boy commented that his mother had told him never to marry a girl who couldn't make a soufflé. I was not planning to marry anyone at that time, but the blow fell hard.

In the years since, I have read the pros and cons of greasing the pan, of low versus high versus high-then-low temperatures for baking, and many other practical fine points of the art of soufflé making.

Nobody has to fail at matrimony because of a sunken soufflé. Here are the rules that work, at least for me.

(1) Use a standard porcelain, 8-cup soufflé dish with straight sides. Butter both sides and bottom, and then dust lightly with flour, or sugar if it's a dessert soufflé. Confectioners' sugar works better than granulated.

> Always break eggs one at a time into a container like a teacup. That way, if a tiny piece of the shell falls in, you can remove it fairly easily. You can also separate eggs more easily if you break them one by one into a cup. If one yolk breaks, that egg can be discarded without ruining an entire soufflé.

(2) Use 5 egg yolks and 6 egg whites: That extra white will make a difference. They should be at room temperature. Separate them carefully; you know that if you get even the tiniest bit of yolk in the whites, they won't whip up, so be very careful. The yolks must be well

The best way to separate eggs, really and truly, is in your hand. Get out a little bowl for the yolks and a bigger one for the whites. Crack the egg on a heavy bowl or the counter rim, hold it over the top of the big bowl, and break it into your palm, then spread your fingers just enough to let the white run through until only the yolk remains. Gently dump the yolk into the small bowl.

beaten, and the whites beaten not too stiff: just swoopy and glossy, but never dry.

(3) Preheat your oven. Set it halfway between 325°F and 350°F. Be sure it is thoroughly heated before the soufflé goes in.

(4) Begin with a hot cream sauce: 3 Tbsp. butter and 3 Tbsp. flour, stirred until smooth over low heat. Add 1 cup milk or half and half (or other liquid if it seems appropriate, like chicken broth for a mushroom soufflé); stir it continuously until it is thick and smooth.

(5) To finish the cream sauce, pour a small amount into the yolks and beat furiously. Pour the yolks into the hot cream sauce and beat until thickened and smooth. A whisk is good for this. Set aside to cool.

(6) Whatever else you add should not exceed 1 cup. Grated cheese melted then cooled, grated semisweet chocolate or chocolate chips, chopped asparagus tips, chopped ham or other meat, coarsely ground peanuts, 1 cup seasoned chopped broccoli, 1 cup prepared morels. Remember: It can't be too heavy for the egg whites to hold up.

(7) The last step is folding in the egg whites. First put a big spoonful of them on top of the cooled cream sauce with the other ingredients already in it. Fold it in to lighten the sauce. Then pour the whole thing over the rest of the whites, and gently fold everything together. Bake in a preheated oven for 40 minutes to 1 hour, until the center is firm.

Pizza

First, preheat the oven to 450°F. Assemble your food processor, 1 envelope rapid-rise dry yeast, ½ tsp. sugar, ½ tsp. salt, about 3 cups unbleached all-purpose flour or bread flour. (You can substitute about ½ cup semolina flour *or* ¾ cup whole wheat flour. You can put up to ¾ cup whole wheat flour in the dough, but more than that destroys the glutinous quality that bread and semolina flour give, and makes the crust brittle, heavy, and hard instead of flexible and chewy.) Mix yeast, sugar, salt, and 1 cup of the flour in the processor. With the machine running, add 1 cup hot (120–130°F) water, and mix. Stop the machine, add another cup of the flour, and run it again. Then begin adding flour a little at a time with the machine running, until the dough balls up into a single lump. After that, run the processor for 2 whole minutes, adding 1 tsp. flour each time the dough ball starts to stick to the sides. This replaces kneading.

I bought my pizza tile at a carpet store. It's a 14" × 14" bathroom tile that had been discontinued, and it cost a dollar. I reasoned that any glazed tile will not crack at a mere 500°F, and I was right. So I preheat it in the oven. I use a pizza peel, a thin wooden paddle with a longish handle on which you make the pizza (flour it first), then gently shuffle the pizza off onto the hot tile when you're ready to cook it.

Turn the dough into a warm, dry bowl that's been oiled with a few drops of olive oil, cover with a cloth, and let rise 10 minutes or so. Punch the dough down, roll it again into a ball.

Sprinkle the counter with 1 Tbsp. flour or cornmeal, and pat the ball out into a flat circle. Sprinkle a little flour over it, and roll dough out from the center with a rolling pin or a straight-sided wine bottle. When it gets to about 14" across, move it to a baking sheet that you've sprayed ahead of time with vegetable spray, or to a floured wooden pizza peel. (Some folks sprinkle the pizza pan or tile with cornmeal, but I don't.) Straighten it up if it has gotten lopsided. Now, with the heel of your hand, nudge the dough from the middle out toward the edges to form the "lip" of the pizza. Bake it 3 minutes in the center of the oven *before* putting the toppings on. This keeps it crisp.

Now you're ready to decorate and bake it. Top the pizza *lightly*. Bake until the cheese melts and the edges turn brown. Watch it carefully so that it doesn't burn. I find scissors cut hot pizza more easily than a pizza roller-cutter.

Quiche

For a basic quiche process, you need a raw pie shell, about 1 cup cheese on the bottom to keep that lower crust from getting soggy, other ingredients layered on next, a custard of 1 egg for every ½ cup milk or half and half, poured in next, and cheese on top. Skim milk can be used, with 1 Tbsp. flour for thickening, but the result is not as creamy. Evaporated skim milk used without dilution is a good compromise. Bake 1 hour or so in the middle of a medium-heat oven (350–375°F). Quiches can be made with wild greens, gently steamed, crisp bacon or fat-free ham, milkweed blooms, and many other things. You are limited only by your imagination.

Piecrust

The best method I know for making piecrust is in a food processor. This makes two crusts, for a two-crust pie or two one-crust pies. In the processor, put 3 cups all-purpose flour and ½ tsp. salt, and whiz it around to mix the salt in. With the machine running, add 1 cup cold shortening in chunks *(not butter or oil or margarine)*. (By the way, do this by putting 1 cup ice water in a 2-cup measure, then adding shortening until the water rises to the 2-cup mark. Drain off the water. You will then have 1 cup shortening. This is far easier than laboriously pushing cold shortening down into a cup, and making sure there are no airholes or spaces.) When it is grainy and well mixed, beat together in a small bowl ½ cup ice water with 1 egg yolk, and add it with the processor running. At once the crust will bunch up into a ball. Stop the processor, divide the dough in half, and roll out each half on a floured board with a floured roller, turning it to keep it roughly round. Roll the circle out gently until it's 1" wider all around than your pie pan. Fold it lightly in half, then again in half, and gently lift the resulting triangle into the pie pan, where you will then unfold it. Prick it, trim the edges and press in fork tines, if you want, to make a pretty edge. Or you can mold the edges by pinching them up into a nice design. Fold the second one the same way before placing it on top of the filling. This is the only piecrust you will ever need. Once you learn the process, you'll never again have to look it up. For some reason, this crust is foolproof. It's the only one I know that won't get soggy or tough, and I'm not deft at pastry.

Baking Mix

My years of scouting and camping taught me a lot, from swimming to square dancing, from camp songs to camp cooking. I remember that there was circulated one year a recipe for a baking mix to speed up cooking, especially useful for Girl Scouts (and others) on cookouts. The idea is to make it ahead of time, then use it as you need it. Store it in 2-cup quantities in the freezer.

> Far easier than a glass dipped in flour to cut round biscuits is *square biscuits:* Pat the dough gently into a ½"-high square, and slice across it quickly with a knife to make 2" strips, then slice across it the other direction to make 2" squares. Just as delicious, and saves time.

Mix 8 cups flour, 3 cups nonfat dry milk, 5 Tbsp. sugar, 5 Tbsp. baking powder, 1 Tbsp. salt, and 1 lb. (2 cups) shortening, *or* 1¾ cups vegetable oil. Blend it together well with knives or a pastry blender until it's the consistency of cornmeal. Store it in the refrigerator. Now here are some things you can do with it:

Biscuits: 2 cups mix, with around ⅓ cup water to just dampen it enough to hold together. Knead only a few strokes, pat to ½", and cut out biscuits. Bake at 400°F for 10 minutes. (For **Stick Biscuits**, add enough water to make it sticky, then mold some of the batter around a green, safe branchlet, and cook it on all sides over a fire, remove the stick, then fill the hole where the stick had been with homemade Wild Jam or Quince Marmalade.)

Indian Fry Bread: Fry those biscuits in ½" vegetable oil, turning once to fry the other side. Serve with homemade Maple Syrup.

Wild Onion Biscuits: 2 cups mix, ½ cup chopped wild onions, and about ⅓ cup water. Mix together, pat out, cut, and bake at 400°F for about 10 minutes.

Wild Berry Muffins: 2 cups mix, 1 egg beaten into ½ cup water, a little additional sugar if you like them sweet, 1 cup berries. Add 1 or 2 drops vanilla, if you like. Mix lightly until just blended, and bake in greased muffin tins at 400°F for about 20 minutes.

Blueberry Pancakes: 2 cups mix, 1 egg, and about ¾ cup water, or enough to make batter the consistency you like. Mix, pour on a hot griddle greased with oil, butter, margarine, or bacon grease, and scatter blueberries thickly onto the batter. Turn once when the bottom side is brown.

Wild fruit Pudding: 2 cups mix, 1 cup sugar, 2 eggs, ¼ cup water, and 2 cups fruit (canned, fresh, or frozen). Preheat oven to 375°F. Grease a baking pan or casserole. Pour the fruit on the bottom, and top with the other ingredients, mixed. Bake for 35 to 40 minutes, until done.

Corn Bread: 2 cups mix, 1 cup cornmeal, 2 eggs, and about 1 cup water. Mix thoroughly, and bake in a greased skillet (bacon grease is best) or baking pan for about 45 minutes at 375°F.

Coffee Cake: 2 cups mix, ⅓ cup sugar, 1 egg, ½ cup water. Beat egg and water together, then quickly stir in mix plus sugar. Don't overstir. Pour into buttered square baking pan, and add a topping before cooking.

Here are some suggestions for toppings: Wild nut topping: 1 cup coarsely chopped nuts tossed with 1 cup brown sugar, ½ stick butter melted, and maybe a dusting of spice like cinnamon or nutmeg, allspice or ginger, or maybe a combination? Crumb topping: 4 Tbsp. butter, 6 Tbsp. flour, 6 Tbsp. sugar, then a little spice. Mix with fork until crumbly. Fruit topping: 1 or 2 cups fruit tossed with half as much sugar and melted butter.

Forager's Don't-Throw-Out-Those-Bananas Bread: 2 cups mix, ⅓ cup sugar, 1 egg, 1 or 2 bananas past prime, mashed, vanilla, and enough water to make a smooth batter. Beat thoroughly, and bake in a loaf pan about 1 hour at 375°F.

Wild Apple Beer Bread: 2 cups mix, 2 Tbsp. sugar, 1 cup chopped apple or applesauce, and enough beer to make a medium batter. Bake in a loaf pan about an hour at 375°F.

Nut Sugar Cookies: 2 cups mix, 1 cup sugar, 2 small eggs or 1 large, ⅓ cup water, ½ cup wild nuts, and 1 tsp. vanilla. Mix, drop by tsp. onto a greased cookie sheet, and bake about 10 minutes at 375°F. Sprinkle with sugar (and cinnamon, if you like) or gelatin dessert right out of the package when they come out of the oven.

Huckleberry Cookies: 2 cups mix and 1 cup or more huckleberries, stirred together. Add the following, mixed: 1 egg, ½ stick butter or margarine, melted, ½ cup each white and brown sugar, 2 Tbsp. water, 2 tsp. vanilla.

Brownies: 1 cup mix, 1 cup light brown sugar, ½ cup cocoa, 1 cup chopped wild nuts, mixed. Add ¼ cup vegetable oil, 1 tsp. vanilla, and 2 eggs, all beaten together. Stir briefly to mix, and bake at 350°F for 25 minutes.

Come on now, your turn! Fig nut bread? You can wing it with this basic helper.

Cream Sauce

Cream sauce may be made thin, medium, or thick. It may be light, medium, or very rich. Cream sauce involves butter or margarine, flour, and a liquid. The process is to melt the butter, stir in the flour for at least 1 minute, to overcome a "floury" taste, and slowly stir in the liquid. Never stop stirring until the sauce is smooth and thickened. The list below shows you the options. Add salt and pepper to taste.

For thick sauce: 2 Tbsp. fat, 2 Tbsp. flour, 1 cup liquid.

For thin sauce: 1 Tbsp. fat, 1 Tbsp. flour, 1 cup liquid.

For fat-free sauce: 2 Tbsp. flour stirred in the dry pan, 1 cup liquid.

For rich sauce: fat, flour, and cream.

For medium sauce: fat, flour, and whole milk or evaporated skim milk.

For light sauce: fat, flour, and skim milk or broth.

For rich but fat-free sauce: flour and evaporated skim milk.

BIBLIOGRAPHY

Agricultural Research Service of the United States Department of Agriculture. *Common Weeds of the United States*. New York: Dover, 1971.

Allegro, John. *The Sacred Mushroom and the Cross*. New York: Doubleday, 1970.

Baikov, Apollonovich. *In the Wilds of Manchuria*. Harbin, China: private printing, 1934.

Buist, Robert. *The Family Kitchen Gardener*. New York: C. M. Saxton and Company, 1857.

Bumgarner, Marlene Anne. *The Book of Whole Grains*. New York: St. Martin's Press, 1976.

Burriss, E. E., and Lionel Casson. *Latin and Greek in Current Use*. New York: Prentice-Hall, Inc., 1939.

Burt, Alison. *Preserves & Pickles*. London: Octopus Books, Ltd., 1973.

Duke, James. *Field Guide to Medicinal Plants*. New York: Houghton-Mifflin Co., n.d.

Emboden, William. *Bizarre Plants*. New York: Macmillan, 1974.

Embury, Emma C. *American Wild Flowers in Their Native Haunts*. New York: D. Appleton & Co., 1845.

Farmer, Fannie Merritt. *The Boston Cooking School Cookbook*. Boston: Little, Brown, and Co., 1936.

Fernald, M. L. *Gray's Manual of Botany, Eighth Edition*. New York: American Book Company, 1950.

Foster, F. Gordon. *Ferns to Know and Grow*. New York: Hawthorn Books, 1971.

Fuller, Andrew S. *The Small Fruit Culturist*. New York: Orange Judd & Co., 1874.

Gibbons, Euell. *Stalking the Faraway Places*. New York: David McKay, 1973.

———. *Stalking the Healthful Herbs*. New York: David McKay, 1966.

———. *Stalking the Wild Asparagus*. New York: David McKay, 1962.

The Gourmet Cookbook, Vol. I. New York: Gourmet Distributing Corporation, 1950.

Gupton, Oscar, and Fred Swope. *Trees and Shrubs of Virginia*. Charlottesville: University Press of Virginia, 1981.

Hamerstrom, Frances. *Wild Food Cookbook*. Ames, Iowa: Iowa State University Press, 1989.

Harding, A. R. *Ginseng and Other Medicinal Plants*. Columbus, Ohio: private printing, n.d.

Harris, Ben Charles. *Better Health with Culinary Herbs*. New York: Weathervane Books, 1971.

———. *Eat the Weeds*. Barre, Massachusetts: Barre Publishers, 1971.

Hatfield, Audrey Wynne. *How to Enjoy Your Weeds*. New York: Collier Books, 1971.

Hitchcock, Susan Tyler. *Gather Ye Wild Things*. Charlottesville: University Press of Virginia, 1980.

Kimmens, Andrew C. *Tales of the Ginseng*. New York: William Morrow and Company, 1975.

Kluger, Marilyn. *The Wild Flavor*. New York: Coward McCann & Geoghegan, Inc., 1970.

Kumin, Maxine. *Up Country*. New York: Harper & Row, 1972.

Leach, Peter, and Anne Mikkelsen. *Malfred Ferndock's Morel Cookbook*. Dennison, Minnesota: Ferndock Publishing, 1986.

Levy, Juliette de Bairacli. *Common Herbs for Natural Health*. New York: Schocken Books, 1966.

Logden, Gene. *Small-scale Grain Raising*. Emmaus, Pennsylvania: Rodale Press, 1977.

Lord, William G. *Blue Ridge Parkway Guide*. Conshohocken, Pennsylvania: Eastern Acorn Press, 1982.

Lyle, Katie Letcher. *The Wild Berry Book*. Minocqua, Wisconsin: NorthWord Press, 1994.

Mabey, Richard. *The New Age Herbalist*. New York: Collier, 1988.

Mann, Rink. *Backyard Sugarin'*. Taftsville, Vermont: The Countryman Press, 1976.

McIntosh, Charles. *Greenhouse*. London: Wm. S. Orr & Co., 1838.

McPhail, Mrs. C. C. *FFV Receipt Book*. Richmond: West, Johnston & Co., 1894.

Miller, Orson K., Jr. *Mushrooms of North America*. New York: Dutton, n.d.

Morse, Sidney. *Household Discoveries*. Petersburg, New York: Success Company's Branch Offices, 1908.

Nagel, Werner O. *Cy Littlebee's Guide to Cooking Fish and Game.* Missouri Department of Conservation. n.d.

Nearing, Helen, and Scott Nearing. *The Maple Sugar Book.* New York: Schocken Books, 1950.

Newman, John B., M.D. *The Illustrated Botany.* New York: J. K. Wellman, 1846.

Parsons, Frances Theodora. *How to Know the Ferns.* New York: Dover, 1961.

Perl, Lila. *The Delights of Apple Cookery.* New York: Bonanza Books, 1963.

Peterson, Lee Allen. *Edible Wild Plants.* Boston: Houghton-Mifflin, 1977.

Pond, Barbara. *A Sampler of Wayside Herbs.* New York: Crown Publishers, 1974.

Rombauer, Irma, and Marion Becker. *The Joy of Cooking.* New York: Bobbs-Merrill, 1951.

Rorer, Sarah T. *Mrs. Rorer's Cook Book.* Philadelphia: Arnold and Company, 1895.

Schwabe, Calvin W. *Unmentionable Cuisine.* Charlottesville: University Press of Virginia, 1979.

Smith, Alexander H. *The Mushroom Hunter's Field Guide, Revised and Enlarged.* Ann Arbor: University of Michigan Press, 1966.

Smith, William J. "Morels." From *The Hollins Poets,* edited by Louis D. Rubin Jr. Charlottesville: University Press of Virginia, 1967.

Strong, A. B., M.D. *The American Flora.* New York: Green & Spencer, 1851.

Stuart, Malcolm, Ed. *The Encyclopedia of Herbs and Herbalism.* New York: Crescent Books, 1979.

Taylor's Guide to Trees. New York: Houghton-Mifflin, 1988.

Thomas, William Sturgis. *Field Book of Common Mushrooms.* New York: G. P. Putnam's Sons, 1928.

Torrey, John. *Natural History of New York.* Albany: Carol and Cook, Printers to the Assembly. 1843.

Vegetable Substances Used for the Food of Man. New York: Harper & Brothers, 1844.

Weiss, Gaea, and Shandor Weiss. *Growing and Using the Healing Herbs.* Emmaus, Pennsylvania: Rodale Press, 1985.

Wilcox, Estelle W. *The New Dixie Cook-book.* Atlanta: Dixie Cook-book Publishing Co., L. A. Clarkson and Co., 1895.

Williamson, Darcy. *How to Prepare Common Wild Foods.* McCall, Idaho: Darcy Williamson Publisher, 1978.

INDEX